D1606938

Broken Glass

George Simms, M.D.

Broken Glass
Copyright © 2024 by George Robert Simms, M.D.

For permission requests, write to the publisher at the address below:
George Simms, M.D.
Masonic Village, Elizabethtown, PA 17022

ISBN 9798345100639

First Edition: November 2024

Printed in the United States of America

Disclaimer
This book is a work of nonfiction. While the author has made every effort to ensure accuracy, this book is not intended as a substitute for professional advice. Readers should consult relevant professionals as needed. The author and publisher disclaim responsibility for any adverse effects resulting directly or indirectly from the information presented in this book.

Acknowledgements

This book would not have come to published fruition without the encouragement and persistence of Kimberly Myers, Ph.D. and Pulkit Bose, M.D.—both of whom recognized the value of my reflections and worked very hard to overcome my hesitancy and fear that my thoughts and insights were of but limited value. To these two faithful friends, I express heartfelt gratitude.

I am also thankful to Christopher Carroll Smith, Ph.D. for his technical help in publishing this manuscript.

Preface

This book is the work of an older man as he reflects on his personal and professional journey as a physician. Such reflections may have little value for those busily immersed in the first half of life. But by the time one reaches middle age and beyond, it becomes clear that life is bittersweet. Bitter because of changes that inevitably accompany the aging process, and sweet if one can find meaning and beauty in the imperfection, awkwardness, and impermanence of it all.

To tell my story, I have used aphorisms of famous and not-so-famous people because they represent the distilled wisdom of a wide range of cultures dating from antiquity to the present. Perhaps I am also drawn to aphorisms because of Winston Churchill's comment that "when you don't have wisdom of your own, you can always borrow someone else's." After each adage, I have written a short reflection in my attempt to understand the wisdom imbedded in each one. As such, this book doesn't have an over-arching narrative. But taken together, the ruminations reveal my struggle to come to grips with what I perceive as the major themes of aging.

A word about the reflections themselves. They were written over several years with no thought of arranging them thematically or chronologically. Each reflection stands by itself as an expression of something I was dealing with at the time. As I pondered the question, an aphorism would come to mind and I would sit down and write about it without censoring it, revising it, or sharing it. As a result, you will find that certain sayings and themes are repeated. This is not by design, but rather how the mind works as it encounters complex problems. Namely, we have a thought, explore it, move on, and return to it later, sometimes understanding it in a new way because of the life we have lived since we last contemplated it—a process that, in educational philosophy, is called "spiraling".

This book is not designed to be read quickly. I invite you to read each reflection slowly and meditatively, asking the same question I did: Is there something here for me to learn about myself?

GRS

Look…isn't that odd

glass shines brighter

when it is broken…

I never noticed that.

Leonard Bernstein: "Mass"

In 1971 Jacqueline Onassis Kennedy asked the American composer Leonard Bernstein to compose a work for the inauguration of the John F. Kennedy Center in Washington, D.C. From that commission came his famous work "Mass, A Theatre Piece for Singers, Players, and Dancers." Imbedded in the opera is a scene where a large pane of glass falls to the ground and is shattered into a thousand pieces. Observing this disaster, a young priest observes: "Isn't that odd. Glass shines brighter when it is broken. I never noticed that."

The broken glass is an eloquent metaphor for life. Sooner or later, we are all broken by the exigencies of life. As Ernest Hemingway once said: "The world breaks everyone." The beautiful pane of glass, once resplendent in its beauty, now lies shattered beyond repair—never to be the same again. A body broken by disease, a mind tortured by stress and tragedy, a marriage fractured beyond reconciliation, a family torn asunder, a career filled with heartbreak and disillusion—in all this we are robbed of our innocence and beauty and lie humbled in disarray.

The power and meaning of this story is that the shattered pieces of broken life exhibit a beauty all their own. If we can get beyond the ugliness we see in ourselves and others, we can catch glimpses of a special beauty that lies (sometimes deep) beneath the surface—a beauty that comes from suffering itself.

The other half of Hemingway's quote is this: "Then some of us get stronger in the broken areas." Hemingway knew more than just that life breaks us. Every cynic knows that. Rather, he knows that it is the brokenness itself that creates the seedbed for inner growth. It is the mysterious alchemy of strength flowing from weakness. This is what the young priest discovers.

Have you ever noticed that those who have suffered greatly often radiate inner peace? Glass does shine brighter when it is broken.

What is essential is invisible to the eye.

Antoine de Saint-Exupéry

Growing old is a challenge to human sensibility and cultural aesthetics. As a hospice physician, I care for men and women who are dying. Most are old and die from debility or dementia. Thanks to the wonders of modern biotechnology, they have managed to live well into their eighties or nineties, and now succumb to the ravages of senility and Alzheimer's Disease. Many have survived cancer and coronary by-pass surgery only to lose their minds a few years later. Yesterday's triumph has become today's failure. It is not a pretty picture.

Many of my patients have photographs on the wall: their wedding day, the kids when they were young, the grand kids, retirement. I stand before each photograph wondering about their journey and pondering the discrepancy between the face in the photograph and the person lying before me in the bed. Once upon a time she was young, beautiful, and radiant. Now she is haggard, tired, and deranged. I grieve this loss.

To grow old in our society—especially to grow old with dementia—is to lose your identity, the essence of who you are, and any possibility of contributing to the common good. We care for them because we want to provide the best for our parents and grandparents. The call to filial piety, by caring for the elderly, resides deeply in all societies. Yet ours is somehow different. Because we venerate youth, physical beauty, and intellectual accomplishment, the inevitable loss of those functions is frightening. The aesthetics of our culture make it difficult to see beauty and worth in anything old. And yet ours may be a distorted view of reality. In almost every other culture, the old are not only tolerated, but venerated. Others see beauty where we see ugliness. How is this possible?

Saint Exupéry may be helpful here. He points to a reality that is not visible to the eye. For him, the essence of personhood is not defined by the presence or absence of physical or intellectual attributes. As tragic as the loss may be, it does not eliminate the essence of the human being. This is not an original thought. Every dementia caregiver—either health care provider or family member—knows this to be true. Long after she can no longer express a coherent thought or control her bodily functions, the essence of that person remains intact. What I have found wondrous is how adept family members are at bringing that "essence" to the surface with a smile, a memory, a song, a touch.

To see the beauty hidden in a broken body or mind is to see with the eyes of love and wisdom. Nowhere in our society can this be learned. It can only come from within—from spiritual resources that transcend taste, intellect, and cultural norms. Surely this is a touch of the Divine.

May you live till you die.

Yiddish Saying

As a hospice physician, I have often been challenged by this saying. All my patients die. It is just a matter of time—usually months, often days or weeks—until the disease process runs its course and the vital organs shut down. I try to make their journey as pain-free and their dying as peaceful as I can. That's all I can do. Or is there more?

Over the years, I have learned that a terminal illness does not mean that life ceases to have meaning, purpose, or pleasure. On the contrary, only when one is faced with a life-threatening illness can life take on its fullest meaning, and the deepest roots of humanity be realized.

My hospice patients—more than anyone—have taught me what it means to live until you die. Not all, to be sure. Some live in anger and die in anger; others die as bewildered as they lived; others cannot face the inevitability of their fate and die in denial. But for many, the journey from life to death becomes a journey from death to life. They have accepted—with deep sadness—the reality of their condition and are grateful for whatever comfort I can offer. In their journey into darkness, these patients tap into a reservoir of strength that allows them to truly "live" before they die. How often have I ministered medically to a patient only to come away having been ministered to?

How can you "live" knowing that you have only six months to live? What is it that makes it possible to look into the abyss and decide that life is still worth living? These people know exactly what is going on in their bodies. They are not in denial, nor are they trapped in a fantasy that tells them that suddenly everything is going to be ok. They seem to bring an inner enlightenment to their situation which pre-dated their diagnosis. There is something already formed in their souls that guides them through the dark passage of pain, uncertainty, and fear.

They suffer like the rest of us. They are not spared the agony and anguish of end-stage disease. What sets them apart, however, is their response to their suffering. While hurting deeply, they remain inwardly quiet in the crisis. They don't seek pain in some masochistic way. But neither do they recoil when it comes. They writhe in pain, often feeling that they can't take any more. But within there is something that gives them the strength to bear the unbearable. And here is the point: they accept their suffering as a burden given them for a higher purpose, and they choose to bear that burden as courageously as they can. They look on life as both a gift and a burden to bear and have accepted the cost of walking by faith in their hour of travail.

I have to say that watching such people face death with this kind of faith, courage, fortitude, and peace touches me to the core, and gives me a new understanding of what it means to live till you die. Society has taught me that when everything material (especially your health) is taken from you, life is not worth living. I know different—not just because I believe it, but because I have seen it.

Hope, I have come to believe,
is as vital to our lives
as the very oxygen we breathe.

Jerome Groopman, M.D.

The longer I practice medicine, the more I am persuaded of the wisdom of the above quote by Dr. Jerome Groopman, noted oncologist at Harvard Medical School. In his book **The Anatomy of Hope**, he discusses candidly how it is that some people prevail in the face of severe illness, and others do not. His conclusion—and ultimately his conviction—is that hope is the key ingredient that allows patients and families to survive—and thrive—amidst unbearable suffering. He writes: "For those who have hope, it may help some to live longer, and it will help all to live better."

We live in a time when science has become the state religion, and university hospitals our temples of salvation. There is good reason for this when one considers what science and technology have given us: blood transfusions, antibiotics, cortisone, insulin, immunizations, vaccines, transplant surgery, unparalleled radiographic imaging capability, renal dialysis, etc. Our quality of life—which we have come to take for granted—would be unthinkable without any of these advances. One hundred years ago the average life span for an American male was forty-seven years. Today it is seventy-six years. It is for good reason that we thought that by the end of the twentieth century, we had found the Holy Grail of Eternal Life.

But it has not turned out that way. Today people live longer, but they die more difficult deaths. One hundred years ago people died swiftly from acute infections, heavy farm equipment injuries, poor nutrition and poor ventilation. With the help of antibiotics, good nutrition, fresh air, immunization, and good education, those scourges no longer plague us. Instead, we die from heart disease, cancer, lung disease, stroke and dementia—all chronic diseases of aging.

What are the lessons here?

1. We have not entered the golden age of perpetual good health

2. Life is still filled with joy and sorrow

3. In the mystery of living life to its fullest, each of us has to find a way to take problems that threaten to crush us, and turn them into challenges that allow us to grow. For this, we need hope

I like Dr. Groopman's definition of hope: "Hope is the elevating feeling we experience when we see—in the mind's eye—a path to a better future." Hope doesn't deny reality. Things are what they are. But hope doesn't allow present circumstances—as disastrous as they may be—to have the final word about the future. In a mysterious way, hope allows one to face the most painful realities of life while at the same time providing the capacity to surmount them.

It's hard to have hope in the midst of depression, a very sick kid, a job loss, or financial insecurity. Yet the truth is, when we allow ourselves to be defined by our circumstances, we relinquish a God-given ability to see beyond the immediacy of the problem. Once the "it" of the problem becomes "us," we get trapped in a mindset which allows the problem to become who we are. Once that happens, we have redefined ourselves to ourselves and to the world.

There is no greater need for hope than raising a child. It is in their early years that children learn to grow in ways that either nurture or negate hope. Parents who are themselves fearful, anxious, and negative make it impossible for their children to grow up with hope. Kids, by nature, mimic, and eventually adopt, the values of their parents. They watch us carefully and pick up our non-verbal cues in everyday circumstances. By the time they are five or six, they have become carbon copies of our worst and best traits. Only later—in adolescence and young adulthood—will they decide what to do with those traits. Some they will use for their own foundation. Others—particularly the destructive traits—they will spend their life trying to exorcise.

Dr. Groopman once wrote: "For all my patients, true hope has proved as important as any medication I might prescribe or any procedure I might perform." I would add that this is just as true for parenting. True hope is as important as anything we can give our kids. It is the elixir they will need to grow and survive.

After I had finished playing,

He thanked me and said:

'You do not know what you are doing.'

Pablo Casals to Vivien Mackie

There are moments in life when one is brought up short by the realization that one is not as far along as he thought. This quote from Vivien Mackie is an account of her study with the great Spanish cellist Pablo Casals. It was a stunning remark because by the time she auditioned with Casals she was an accomplished cellist, having won first prize in a national cello competition in her native Scotland. Casals went on to say: "I can't even tell if you have any talent. If you are to study with me, we must go back to the beginning."

It is a testimony to Vivien Mackie's intelligence and humility that she embraced Casals' assessment of her ability, and spent the next two years working to unlearn the bad habits she had acquired, and develop new ways of thinking and playing which eventually allowed her to become an outstanding cellist and teacher in her own right.

How is it possible to be good at something, and then be told that you don't really know what you are doing? Of course, you know what you are doing. You've been doing it this way for years—and with success. But is that really what Casals meant? Did he perhaps mean that even though she played all the right notes, she lacked creativity? Is there a difference between being a virtuoso and making music? The two would seem synonymous but aren't. Every good teacher knows that.

Why did this interchange between Pablo Casals and his twenty-one-year-old student catch my attention? Why did I underline it and pen in a few margin notes of my own? Why has it bothered me over the years? The answer, of course, is that I am that student. After so many years of study and experience, I am very accomplished in some areas of my life. But could I withstand the scrutiny of a great teacher? Alas, would Casals say to me: "You do not know what you are doing. You must begin again at the beginning"?

In the biblical story of Christ's prediction that St. Peter will deny him, Jesus says to Peter: "Once you have retraced your steps, strengthen your brothers." It is the willingness to "retrace" in the midst of self-assurance that is so difficult, and yet often so necessary, if one is to continue to grow. T.S. Eliot put his finger on the reason when he said:

Humility is the most difficult of all virtues to achieve; nothing dies harder than the desire to think well of oneself.

Most people's lives I write about
are dull, simple, amazing, unfathomable –
deep caves paved with kitchen linoleum.

Alice Munro

This comment, by esteemed novelist Alice Munro, took my breath away. With the keen eye and sensibility of a writer, she has discerned one of the abiding truths of life—namely, beneath the surface of most people's lives there exists another, often richer dimension of their personality which remains hidden until someone discovers it. In her words, "deep caves paved with kitchen linoleum." I love her word imagery: "deep caves," "paved," "kitchen linoleum." It all points to a depth hidden beneath the exigencies of everyday life. When I think about this, I'm convicted by how many people I have encountered and never realized how much more there was to them than I thought.

The kitchen linoleum is the persona we construct as a way to survive, to achieve, or protect ourselves from the grief and pain of previous hurts. It is the necessary coat of armor we wear in order to "make it" in this dangerous and troubled world into which we were born. As necessary as it is, our persona can become a liability when one of two things happens:

1. When a life trauma is so great that it threatens to destroy us (and who can say what "trauma" is for another person?). Over time, we develop an outer psychological exterior (a persona) which allows us to get on with life without being destroyed by the pain that produced the trauma. The development of the persona is not so much a conscious decision as it is a slow, unconscious process which accrues over time. Eventually we lose touch with the pain (Munro's "deep cave") as we learn to

adjust and accommodate to the exigencies of life (her "kitchen linoleum"). But vestiges (voices from the cave) remain subtle, repetitive warning signals in our thinking or behavior, which we can choose to ignore or explore. To ignore the signs is easier and more expedient but has a high cost. To pay attention and ask what it all means is more painful but holds the promise of healing and integration of our personality.

2. When we so invest ourselves in our persona, we become the image we want the world to see. This is a danger for all of us. Everyone wants to be loved and liked. It's simply a part of who we are. But if the "nice me" is not balanced by an awareness that I am more than that air-brushed portrait of myself I need you to believe, I fall prey to a dangerous self-delusion.

Shankar Vedantam's book *Useful Delusions* speaks directly to this point—namely we all create stories we tell ourselves about ourselves in order to enhance our position in the world. In Vedantam's view, this very human trait is useful up to a point. But when it becomes a substitute for who we really think we are, it has become a farcical—and dangerous—liability.

The point of all this is that we are both "kitchen linoleum" and "deep caves." We are both exposed and hidden, light and dark, beautiful and ugly. It is not an either/or construct. We are capable of simultaneously doing great good and great harm. When we value one component over the other, we run the danger of suppressing the opposite side, and eventually repress it beyond recognition. At that point, we have entered the realm of self-delusion.

I am also astonished by another aspect of Alice Munro's comment—namely, the people she writes about (and most of her writing centers on people in her small town) live lives that are dull yet fascinating, simple yet complex, uninteresting yet very interesting. This is the point: their lives—and our lives—

are both. So-called uninteresting people have very interesting, oft hidden, personal lives that become visible only if one gets to know them well enough to discover that part of them. Getting to know someone in the privacy of their life requires both time and trust. We will only divulge the deeper part of ourselves to someone who has earned our trust by spending time to get to know us in a sincere, authentic way, and someone whom we believe can handle the deeper secrets hidden away in our caves. This level of self-disclosure is made more difficult if one has had their trust betrayed earlier in life. For these, the door can perhaps no longer be opened. It is simply too painful.

I never cease to be amazed at the pain and suffering most people bear in their hearts as they shuffle silently through life. Most of that pain remains hidden because there is no one who hears that still, small voice in their "deep cave."

The American writer Willa Cather was right when she wrote:

> *The heart of another is a dark forest, always,*
> *no matter how close it has been to one's own.*

Grief is the price we pay for love.

Anonymous

I have recently had an experience—in this case monetary loss—which brought home the truth of this saying. What I learned is that there are times when good intentions have bad outcomes. Life is strange, quirky, and unpredictable. The best laid plans can go awry in ways that create surprise, disappointment, loss, disfavor—and worse. Sometimes one can look back and see one's mistakes. Other times, not. The temptation is always to blame oneself, the other person, bad circumstances, or bad karma. The trick is to review objectively what happened, identify (if possible) what went wrong, accept responsibility for one's part, avoid unnecessary introspection, and move on.

The deeper issue is the relationship between grief and love. The suffering that inexplicably accompanies love has been explored by all the great thinkers—both ancient and modern. The literature is vast because the experience is universal. The grief imbedded in love is not, in any way, to denigrate love. Without love we would not be human, and life would not be worth living. Love, expressed in its fullest dimension, is the single greatest transformative gift in the world. But when love comes to the heart, it brings with it the specter of grief. The Romans understood this in creating the god Janus who was identified as the god of doors, gates, and all beginnings, and is represented artistically with two identical but opposing faces. To be Janus-faced in our nomenclature is to have two contrasting aspects—usually positive or negative. That's the way love is. It has two contrasting aspects: joy and sorrow. We all want the joy and fear the sorrow. That's understandable, but unfortunately impossible. The two are somehow woven into the DNA of human relationships and cannot be torn asunder.

The Irish poet David Whyte knows this to be true of all friendship. He writes:

All friendships of any length are based on continued, mutual forgiveness. Without tolerance and mercy, all friendship dies.

Intimacy—physical, intellectual, emotional, spiritual—is our greatest need because it is only in intimacy that we find our greatest longings fulfilled.

But what is intimacy? Henri Nouwen gave the perfect definition:

Intimacy is the fruit that grows through touching one another's wounds.

It is natural to avoid grief. It is supernatural to give ourselves to a love which accepts (and embraces) the reality of hurting as the price we pay for love.

Youth is full of pleasure,

Age is full of care.

William Shakespeare: "Julius Caesar"

To know how to grow old
is the masterwork of wisdom, and one of the
most difficult chapters in the art of living.

Henri-Frederic Amiel

Yesterday I attended the funeral service for one of my neighbors—a dear, sweet man who lived down the hall from me. I came to know Art over the years and held him in great affection. On the frontispiece of the funeral service bulletin was a picture of Art as a WWII Army officer—young, dashing, resolute, filled with energy. That was the Art I never knew. The Art I knew was old, sad, stooped over, walking slowly with a cane, speaking softly only when asked a question. I had the privilege of helping him into hospice during his last days. The sadness of it all came back to me as I stared at the bulletin, thinking how strange and pointless it is that we end our days in such predictable decrepitude and pain.

As rich as these last years of my life have been, I am aware that this is not the way many spend the wintertime of their life. Though I have had my share of health problems, I am in remarkably good health and able to enjoy a wide range of fulfilling activities. If I were in chronic pain or immobilized by a severe stroke or dementia, things would be different. Shakespeare was right: "Age is full of care." Yet that cannot be the last word to be said about the "slings and arrows of outrageous fortune." Of equal importance is the attitude with which we face the vicissitudes of aging and loss.

Here, the Swiss philosopher Henri Amiel has something important to say. Growing old is a biologic "given." Growing old wisely is something else. To be sure, it is difficult. As I sat looking at the funeral bulletin, it took every bit of strength not to give in to the depressive awareness that I, too, may end up like Art: broken in body and spirit, isolated and bereft.

What is the "masterwork of wisdom" Amiel is referring to? To know that is to conquer the sting of death that St. Paul alludes to in I Cor. 15:55: confusion, helplessness, fear, anger, despair, self-pity, and the inability to let go and move on.

We have each to find our own wisdom—that encounter with life that gives us meaning and hope and enables us to bear the pain and perplexity of our humanity within a context that knows—and embraces—both joy and suffering. To find that wisdom is difficult and, paradoxically, the most important task of aging.

Lord, teach us to number our days,

that we may apply our hearts unto wisdom.

Psalm 90:12

Our worth is not the same as our usefulness

Henri Nouwen

Most of my hospice patients are old and demented. Men and women in their eighties and nineties who babble incoherently, incontinent of urine and stool, have to be fed, who have nothing to say and nothing to look forward to. They consume enormous health care resources and offer nothing in return. In utilitarian terms, they are useless.

Are they really useless? I used to think so. As a younger physician, I viewed my nursing home patients as bodies to be tended to—men and women who once led robust and vital lives but were now defunct and deficient. I helped them as best I could, but did not invest a lot of time in them as persons. There was nothing there to invest in.

As I have grown, I have changed my attitude—thanks, in part, to Henri Nouwen's distinction between worth and usefulness, and because of my experience with my wife Betty's dementia. I have come to see that I am a child of the culture and attitudinal mindset in which I was raised. In America, if you are old and/or past your peak of effectiveness, you are considered to have lost your usefulness to the greater good of society. We will grudgingly take care of you, but only because it is our duty—not because we see any inherent value in you.

This utilitarian point of view changes as we ourselves grow older, and especially if we have a loved one who becomes "useless." Suddenly we realize that there is more to life than making a contribution, and more to growing old than the sum total of our losses. Inside every frail, elderly person is a human being of worth who has a story to tell. Once I grant worth to my dementia patients, everything changes. The reality of their deficient minds is no longer their sole defining characteristic. Behind a warped mind lies a valuable—and often noble—soul. It is their soul that I must learn to see and honor.

I have discovered that working with the "losers" in society— the elderly, the deformed in body or mind, the poor, and the disenfranchised—is the best way to discover the difference between worth and usefulness. If I get to know one of these people well enough, if they trust me enough to tell me their story, I discover the richness, as well as the impoverishment, of their journey. More important, I see myself in the other. His dreams, hopes, and fears are the same as mine. It is only the accidents of biology, family life, educational opportunities, and the presence of friends and mentors along the way that have made the difference in our lives. Once the facade of failure, disease, and age has been stripped away, I realize that he is as worthy—and deserves as much respect—as I.

Those who have not suffered have orthodox answers.

Those who have suffered no longer have orthodox answers.

Robert Gordis

I am constantly amazed at how the exigencies of life change the ground rules for how one lives life. This is a truism, of course. But a truism learned only in retrospect. Early on life is simple, the ground rules are clear, the path is straight, and the goals are reachable. It's all rather linear. Except it isn't. Unanticipated failures, disappointments and setbacks contrive to challenge everything you thought you knew about yourself and how you are supposed to live your life.

It was all so clear: work hard in school and become a doctor, marry and raise a family, work hard in my profession and become successful, obey the rules and become a leader in my community, complete my journey with professional esteem and personal satisfaction. There is nothing wrong with this plan—except it didn't work out. It didn't work out because it was an illusion, a caricature of what life is. Looking back, I understand what the Egyptian writer Naguib Mahfouz meant when he said,

The loss of an illusion became a source of strength.

So much of life is an illusion because we don't know how to deal with suffering. Suffering, as it strikes us so hard and unexpectedly, is an essential ingredient of life. Against our will, it changes—sometimes drastically—who we are and what we become.

Moving from orthodoxy to unorthodoxy is tricky business. One of the great blessings of life is having a foundation— emotional, spiritual, and intellectual—upon which to stand.

This is why parental love and early teaching are so essential to character development. We know who we are because we trusted those who gave us our heritage. But sooner or later, the exigencies of life shake our foundations like tectonic plates moving beneath the ocean. With sudden and overwhelming force, we are confronted with circumstances not of our making. What was once clear is now opaque, what was once unthinkable is now thinkable. Suddenly, we're not so sure what we should do.

To my utter amazement, I don't know where I am going. I used to think I knew. But too much has happened for me to have certainty about anything. My orthodoxy—the simple existential answers that guided me for so many years—has been taken away by the suffering of broken dreams, illness and aging, and has been replaced by an unorthodoxy which is both frightening and liberating.

When someone is not loved, they seek to be admired.

Aristotle

We pride ourselves on understanding human behavior and think that everything prior to Freud was primitive at best. But this observation from Aristotle dispels that assumption.

It is in our DNA to be loved. And it is in our DNA to be admired. The problem is that admiration, by itself, is a poor substitute for love. A child who is loved wants also to be admired but can get along without it as long as she knows that she is truly loved by her parents and family. Where that is not the case, she goes through life seeking admiration as a substitute for love.

The trouble is, it doesn't work. Down deep inside we know that but have no other way of validating ourselves. So we continue to strive for admiration until we become addicted to it. And then it is too late. We are now trapped in a life defined by "external self-validation"—that is, I know that I am good because I make sure that "you" (the world) remind me that I am. The contract is this: I will work hard so that you will grant me your admiration. But the price is high: perfectionism, the curse of the unloved.

Aristotle figured this out three centuries before Christ. The truth is that the basic human condition has not changed since time immemorial. The overwhelming power of love, hate, and fear has been with us from the beginning because it is written into our genetic code. What is different are the different ways societies have tried to deal with these needs.

There is nothing in this world more important than being loved. And there is no one who can give that love better than our parents. In fact, loving our children to the deepest core of their being is the single most important task of parenthood. When we fail at that, we force the child to seek it elsewhere. Why? Because no one can go through life without love.

An obsessive need for admiration is a sign of profound emotional insecurity and is rooted in a longing for true love. In this quest we will use our minds, our bodies, our talents, our hard work, our achievements, our religion, our children. The list goes on and on. Only when we are exhausted and find someone who loves us enough to tell us the truth about ourselves, is there hope for change.

Be kind, for everyone you meet is fighting a hard battle

Plato

I never cease to be amazed at the burdens people bear. Burdens of physical pain, marriage, children, parents, finances, work, unfulfilled personal dreams. Anyone can live with heavy burdens for a short time. But for many, these burdens last a lifetime. And yet they keep on going, doing the best they can, living from day to day, hoping for a little relief, fighting the fear that this is the best it will ever be.

Being a physician has granted me the privilege of listening to countless patients unburden their hearts. What I have discovered is that sooner or later, most people know that not much is going to change. That awareness eventually leads to an existential loneliness that is corrosive to the soul.

When, however, they meet someone who takes time to listen to their story, and appreciates the depth and difficulty of their journey, they are profoundly grateful. It doesn't take the pain away, but it does provide a moment of respite from the emotional isolation. Sometimes that's enough to keep on bearing the burden.

When I was a young physician, I didn't understand why so many patients appreciated a listening ear. But now I understand. I understand because I have lived long enough to experience the mystery of suffering in my own life. Their pain has become my pain. We are fellow sojourners along the path of life.

It is utterly remarkable how well we are able to go through life hiding our pain from the world, and sometimes from ourselves. The public persona we create over the years gets us by quite well. Without that mask, life would be intolerable. We learn early on that it is folly to share our innermost doubts and dilemmas with everyone. Even family and friends often cannot be trusted with this knowledge. So we try to figure out who can be trusted, who has the depth to hear our confessions, and who is committed to walk with us through thick and thin. Sometimes we trust, only to have our trust betrayed. We barricade ourselves behind an elegantly constructed persona that enables us to do what we have to do: go to school, find a job, get married, raise a family, become successful. And no one knows.

Is there a cure for this affliction? Probably not. Our burdens are so interwoven with our genes, our personalities, our family, our society, and our circumstances that radical change is not possible. We are left to do the best we can. Which is why Plato said: "Be kind." By this, he didn't mean the syrupy kind of sympathy that so often passes for kindness. Rather, a quiet sensitivity born of having faced one's own broken dreams. People who have been bowed down by life have a look in their eyes, a sound in their voice, a way of walking and shaking your hand that announces their pain. The language of true suffering cannot be spoken. But it can be understood by a fellow sufferer. Hermann Hesse once wrote:

Only those who are themselves in need of being treated kindly can be gentle and forbearing with others.

Strange how that which is most personal is most universal.

Blessed is he who has found his work.

Let him ask no other blessedness.

Thomas Carlyle

The other day I received a copy of the Harvard University Board of Overseers election list, and the list of candidates for the Harvard Alumni Association Board of Directors. All Harvard graduates are invited annually to cast ballots for these positions—a governance opportunity unique among American colleges and universities.

As I read through the list, I was impressed with the credentials and qualifications of each of the candidates—men and women who have used their education to make significant contributions to their individual communities. Any of these people will serve well.

What struck me even stronger is that being a University Overseer or Board Director—though honorable—is a task for which I am not well suited, and would not be good at. In fact, I'm not well suited to do anything other than what I am doing right now. And herein lies the epiphany: I have found my work—that which suits me by training, temperament, and age—and that suffices.

Our tasks change as we age, mature, and reach new goals. When I look back over the last forty years, I am amazed at the diverse and challenging tasks I undertook—some successful, others less so; some rewarding, others less so. Each step along the way, I thought I was making the right choice. When the choice turned out to be wrong, I wondered where I went wrong—or if I did. Now, with the benefit of age and wisdom, I see it as a tapestry made up of interwoven threads of success and failure. I could not see it at the time, of course; no one can. But now it looks different. The pain, anger, frustration, pride, ecstasy of accomplishment and fear of failure have all burned away. What is left is a kind of serenity that no longer strives to succeed and can accept the mystery of incompleteness and ambiguity.

Which brings me back to my Overseer list and Thomas Carlyle. There is a kind of "blessedness" in doing what you know you should be doing. What I did twenty years ago was right for that time in my life. It was productive and satisfying, though not always successful. But I am not there anymore. What I now do—though reduced in pace and scope—is what I need to do. I think Carlyle would agree.

Finally, at last, one has lived long enough
to see that everything belongs,
even the sad, absurd, and futile parts.

Richard Rohr

As I look back on my life, I'm amazed at how unaware I was of the fact that "everything belongs"—even the absurd, painful, and seemingly futile aspects of life. At the heart of this truth is a perspective that sees life in a larger context than the usual immediacy by which we live our daily lives.

To see life in this larger context requires both time and experience. One has to have lived long enough and tasted in one's flesh (as the French poet Paul Valery would say) all the joys and sorrows of life to know that this is the way it must be. Without the lived experiences of the first half of life—when one must strive to succeed and be willing to pay any price to reach his/her goal—it is impossible to have a context with which to judge one's journey, and to grow deeper.

There is so much in life that is sad, cruel, absurd, and futile. I think of Voltaire's observation:

All history is little more than a long succession of useless cruelties.

This is painfully true. But I don't think I thought about it much in my earlier years. I was too busy trying to survive and do whatever I needed to advance my goals. But now, from the vantage point of more than seventy years, I know that Voltaire was right.

I live in a culture, and at a time, when Rohr's observation makes little sense. It smacks of a passivity that is almost un-American. Given enough time, we can eliminate disease, cruelty, poverty, and all other maladies of life. Look, we conquered tuberculosis and poliomyelitis, didn't we? We put a man on the moon, didn't we? We invented the computer and now have Artificial Intelligence. If we have the will, inventiveness, and technology, the rest will follow. One part of me wants to believe this; the other part knows it is a delusion. To be fully human requires that one face the absurdity and sadness inherent in life, and to recognize that only when we accept the dark side of life can we move to higher ground where we realize that "everything belongs."

While I have spent my life doing what I can to alleviate the suffering of my patients, I have come to realize that life is what it is. In a deep and mysterious way sadness, absurdity, and futility are woven into the fabric of our existence. I may fight it (as I should with the tools at my disposal), but I will not eradicate it. If I am to know joy, I must know sorrow. In the mystery of our humanity, everything belongs.

Kindness is more important than wisdom,
and the recognition of this is the
beginning of wisdom.

Theodore Isaac Rubin

The older I grow, the more important kindness becomes. Courtesy is not the same thing as kindness. Kind people are always courteous. But courtesy alone is based on politeness and nothing more (the cashier in the supermarket who says "Have a nice day" without looking up).

Kindness is more than an action; it is an attitude. It is a way of relating to people in a certain way. Kind people tend to be kind to everyone. A poignant example of this is a Revolutionary War document written by a British soldier wounded in the Battle of Brandywine and cared for on the colonial side by the Sisters of the Solitary in their cloister hospital on Zion Hill. He writes:

I expected to meet with cold reservedness and was surprised by exhibitions of the most charming affability and disinterested benevolence.

It is his phrase "disinterested benevolence" that touches me, for it is this mindset that is crucial in making kindness possible. Benevolence that is "indifferent" is benevolence grounded in a conscious decision to respond to all people regardless of race, gender, age, ethnicity, religious or political persuasion, or past grievances with equality and understanding. It is the moral equivalent of Martin Buber's distinction between an I-It and an I-Thou relationship. When he said, "All real living is meeting," he was describing an encounter based on mutual "disinterested benevolence." That is, meeting based on the inherent goodness of the other.

When I think of kindness, I think of my mother-in-law. She was a woman of limited abilities and simple faith. For over fifty years I disagreed with her views on God, man, politics, and parenting. The simplicity of her theology was maddening. But there was an unalloyed goodness about her that put me to shame. I don't think I ever figured out how she could be so wrong about so many things I thought were important, and so right about the one thing that counts. Hers was the world of house cleaning, going to church, and doing good. But from that sphere radiated an innocence and friendliness that embraced everyone and made her beloved by adults and children alike. That is more than I can say about myself and most of the savants I have traveled with.

Where I come from knowledge is of vital importance in the mission of solving problems. It is only from the great religions of the world that one learns that there is something beyond knowledge—namely, wisdom, that mysterious ability to use knowledge not just to solve problems, but to construct lives that are in harmony with the greater goals of the universe. To move from information gathering to wisdom is to move along a continuum from concrete to abstract, from that which is verifiably true to that which is true but not verifiable.

As if that is not enough, Rubin suggests that beyond wisdom is kindness. This reminds me of Paul Ricouer's idea of a "second naivete." What he meant is that there comes a point—usually in later life—when we return to certain basic concepts—concepts learned earlier in life but discarded—that prove to have lasting value. Often these concepts have to be recast in ways that make them usable at the stage in which we find ourselves. If that can be done, they become powerful guidelines for our lives. For me, kindness is one such. Maybe it is because I am moving toward the end of my journey, and realize that the time will come when my decline will make me dependent on the kindness of others. I see how dependent my wife is on the kindness of the aides who care for her in the nursing home. Their gentleness and compassion makes her life bearable. When I reflect on this, I know Theodore Rubin is right.

Knowledge is to be prized, for without it we have no future. But at the end of the journey, as we enter the valley of the shadow of death, it is kindness that makes the journey possible.

Pay as little attention as you can
to the faults of other people,
and none at all to their natural
defects and eccentricities.

Thomas Merton

Is there anything harder in life than this? I think not. Fault finding is so deeply ingrained in the human heart that to take Merton's admonition seriously almost defies belief. As a matter of fact, the ability to find fault—especially for the educated and successful of the world—is an art form, meticulously developed over the years, that has its own satisfaction and reward.

In writing this, I am describing myself for much of my life. I am quite adept at identifying the flaws in my patients, colleagues, friends, family, and enemies. I am, what might be called, an equal opportunity observer of the frailties, flaws, and foibles of mankind. I am adept at "reading" people quickly and seeing behind their defense mechanisms. While this ability has served me well in some professional settings, it has come at a high price. I found it difficult to accept people without judging their motives, and more important, I became better at seeing their flaws than I did my own. In fact, it took years before I realized that the very flaws I saw in others were the exact ones I harbored but could not recognize.

It wasn't until I began taking seriously Jesus' warning about seeing the speck in the brother's eye and not seeing the beam in my own, that I realized how warped and unloving my own attitude was. In the years since, I have seen how imbedded this trait is, and how it becomes reinforced in everyday interactions. We all have to make judgments about people and things. But we don't have to judge the person in a critical way. Thomas Carlyle struck the right balance on this point when he said:

For all right judgment of any man or thing,

it is essential to see his good qualities

before pronouncing on his bad.

Merton goes even further in two ways: first, by pointing out that "looking away" is a volitional act—something I can choose to do. If I do not make myself look away, I will not look away. Looking away, like any other habit, is hard to do. But it can be done. Second, he makes a distinction between faults and "natural defects and eccentricities." Natural defects and eccentricities are not faults. They are a part of who we are. And while some defects are disconcerting, and some eccentric behavior is at times highly charged and troublesome, we cannot change them any more than we can change our genes, our family, our culture or our upbringing. For these, Merton admonishes us not only to "pay as little attention as you can," but to ignore them.

None of this is easy. In fact, I believe it is well-nigh impossible when spelled out in day-to-day living. The unconscious forces that drive me, when combined with the unconscious forces that drive every person I meet, makes psychic combustion both painful and inevitable. Notwithstanding, I believe that grace can break through the chain of events that drives us to react the way we do, and create breakthroughs and new beginnings. Without this grace, we are cursed to live out Samuel Johnson's prediction:

The chains of habit are too weak to be felt

until they are too strong to be broken.

What do you have that
God hasn't given you?
And if all you have is from God,
why act as though
you are so great,
and as though you have accomplished
something on your own?

I Corinthians 4:7

I'm one of those who hangs pictures and sayings on the wall to remind me of where I've been, and to remind me that there is no such thing as a self-made man. We are all the product of our biology, our family, our culture, and the goodness of others along the way.

As I scan the walls of my study, I am struck by how many doors I knocked on that didn't open. Each was an opportunity I longed for and was heartbroken when that dream didn't come true. By the same token, how many unexpected doors opened which have shaped my life in ways that made me who I am. Where I went to school, what I did for a living, who I married, where I lived, the relationships I formed, the tragedies that engulfed my life, the development of my inner life, how I have lived the last years of my life—none of it turned out the way I planned. What I have learned is that it never does.

There is something offensive—almost un-American—about the Bible verse I quoted. It is deeply imbedded in a Puritan/Calvinistic theology (which has become the American "can-do" spirit) that we can achieve whatever we want if we just try hard enough, and that God rewards those who try hard enough. As laudable as that work ethic may be, it has not worked in my life. Hard work did not open the doors I wanted.

41

By contrast, other unexpected doors opened which took me down quite different paths from the ones I thought I wanted. It is almost as if there has been another, unknown force active in my life to "self-correct" my decisions, and guide me along byways I could not have known. This is the story of my pictures and sayings: men and women who have inspired me over the years, companions to remind me that I stand like a pygmy on the shoulders of great people who have gone on before, and have left their mark on my heart and mind.

A persuaded mind and even a well-intentioned heart

is a long way from exact and faithful practice.

Francois Fenelon

I have this saying hanging on the wall in my music room so I can look at it every time I practice my cello. It is one of the most demanding admonitions I know because it reminds me of a flaw in my character. Though I am well intentioned, I often lack the discipline, courage, and stamina necessary for exact and faithful practice. The old saying "practice makes perfect" is not true. What is true is "perfect practice makes better." Without this, the dream never becomes a reality.

There is something noble and important about working at a task (learning a foreign language, a musical instrument, higher mathematics, fly-fishing, becoming a gourmet chef, etc.) despite doubt, frustration, and discouragement. To do this takes more than talent. To be sure, talent is a great and wonderful gift. But without the discipline of exact and faithful practice, the talent eventually stagnates and drifts into (oft unrecognized) mediocrity. What is left is the perfume of an empty vase.

The challenge I face is what to do when I realize that I am not getting anywhere. I have reached a kind of permanent plateau. Biology is catching up with me in ways that are making it increasingly difficult to play the cello. At seventy-six I have diminishing strength in my left hand, and an intentional tremor in my right arm that makes it difficult to hold the bow. I am tempted to give it up. Yet I still love it.

When you have a persuaded and a sincere heart, but realize that you have reached the limits of your ability, is there any reason to persist in the discipline of exact and faithful practice? Judged on performance capacity alone, the answer is probably "no." Yet I am learning that there is more to performing a difficult task than "performing." When I was a kid, I played in a civic marching band whose motto was "Building Character Through Music." I had no idea what that meant. But now I do. There is something about any task requiring a deep and sustained commitment that creates the foundation for the virtues of patience, endurance, hope, and faith. It is these very virtues that make it possible to endure and flourish in other areas of our lives. In short, it is character building.

Part of me wants to give it up. I'm tired of practicing the same exercises over and over again with no improvement. But in my dejection I know there are lessons to be learned: endurance, attention, and appreciation for the occasional moment of beauty.

Henry Moore, the great British sculptor, was once asked the secret of life. He said:

The secret of life is to devote yourself entirely to one end, to one goal, and to work every day toward this goal, to put all your energy and imagination into one endeavor. The only necessity is that this goal be unattainable.

Learning To Say Goodbye

Since my stroke, which, along with other neurologic deficits, left me with left-sided weakness and tremors, I have been unable to play my beloved cello. After countless attempts to compensate, nothing worked, and so I was left with no choice but to give it up. I have played the cello for over fifty years, and it has been an abiding passion in my life. To be forced to give it up has been like losing a dear friend to death. It has closed an important chapter in my life—against my will.

As much as I mourn this loss, I know that saying goodbye is a part of life. We must all learn how to say goodbye—to dreams, relationships, and activities—in ways that allow us to move on without being paralyzed by regrets for the past and fears for the future. Until we can do this, we remain stuck, and foreclose the opportunity to grow and meet new challenges.

Two pieces of ancient wisdom helped me get through this. The first is the Chinese word for "crisis." The word is made up of two characters: **Danger** and **Opportunity**. In ancient Chinese thinking, a crisis is "a dangerous opportunity." That is, at the heart of the pain and turbulence (the crisis itself) there is the possibility for something new to emerge (the opportunity). Crisis is thus a two-edged sword that both cuts and heals. In trying to work through a crisis, we have the choice of either being consumed by the pain, so that pain becomes our response to life, or searching for the hidden opportunity to find meaning, bring closure, and move on.

The second piece of ancient wisdom is from the biblical Book of Ecclesiastes: "For there is a season, and a time for every matter under heaven." There is a time and place for everything in life. A time to begin and a time to end; a time to start and a time to finish; a time to enter and a time to leave; a time to live and a time to die. To understand life is to understand the rhythms of life. And by the same token, to refuse to acknowledge these rhythms is to create chaos and pain that can rob us of peace and joy.

When is it time to say goodbye to a love affair, a marriage, a job, a child, a place, a specific activity (like playing my cello)? No one can know that for another person. The moment of truth is deeply personal, quietly convincing (though its voice may be suppressed), and ultimately life-changing. When it comes, we are then confronted with a decision to act or not to act. Either way, the choice is ours alone to make.

We think about life retrospectively. That is, it makes sense after the fact. But we live life prospectively. That is, we usually make the big decisions of life without knowing all the facts. For example, should I get married? Should I leave? If I do, what comes next? Should I buy that house? Is this the right college? In trying to answer these questions, we need to listen—and learn to trust—that inner voice that can guide us in ways that might seem counterintuitive or even scary. Saying goodbye works much the same way. If we listen carefully, resist the temptation to censor material we don't want to confront, and have the courage to act on what our heart knows is right, we will be able to close chapters with wisdom, grace, and finality— though it may be painful.

Is the path of closure and transition worth it? No, if comfort, convenience, and avoidance of pain are your main goals. But yes, when you realize that there is a new, challenging, and exciting chapter of life awaiting you. Yes, if you believe that hidden in the danger is opportunity. That thought is hard to hang on to when one is in the midst of darkness, indecision, and turmoil. For this reason, we need to be reminded that when one door closes, another will open. But we will never find that new door until we fully close the old door.

It is the hardest thing in the world to say goodbye to someone—or something—you love. We all face those moments when anguish, guilt, and fear threaten to suck the very life out of us. The only way around it is to go through it. In those moments, you need to know that there is hope beyond grief, joy beyond pain, and life beyond loss. There will be an end to your suffering.

Muss es sein? Es muss sein.

Beethoven String Quartet in F Major, Opus 135

These words ("Must it be? Yes, it must be") were written at the end of the final movement of Beethoven's string quartet, Opus 135. No one knows exactly what he meant by that question. But I have taken it to mean something deeply personal as I have decided to give up playing my beloved cello.

Must it be? Yes, it must be. I can no longer bear the burden of trying to overcome the relentless intention tremor in my right arm, and increasing weakness in my left hand. I have tried every possible way to overcome this impediment, but to no avail. All my ardor, faithfulness, and discipline have not been able to overcome the changes taking place in my body. As I write this, I think of Leon Fleisher, the great American pianist, who lost the use of his right hand at the height of his career. He spent years trying to find a cure—all to no avail. That's how I feel.

The last day I played, I thought of two Bible verses:

The Lord has given, the Lord has taken;
Blessed be the name of the Lord.

Job 1:21

&

For everything there is a season.

Ecclesiastes 3:1

I have played the cello for fifty-two years. In doing so, my life has been immeasurably enriched. Hearing the great French cellist Pierre Fournier perform Dvorak's Cello Concerto in June 1961 was a life-changing experience; through my first

48

Swiss teacher Hans Thomas, I was ushered into the world of Bach. I studied under students of Pablo Casals, Bernard Greenhouse, and Ron Leonard—all masters, and from them I learned what artistic greatness is. That exposure changed how I think about music.

I have put my cello down with gratitude coupled with the sadness that comes from losing an old friend. Though I began studying late (I was 26 years old and in my third year of medical school), I was able to play relatively uncomplicated string trios and quartets, and simple encore pieces. But nothing more. But that was enough to bring me enormous pleasure. Though there is no substitute for talent, I learned that you can go pretty far with dreams, hard work, and enthusiasm.

Thomas Carlyle once said: "There is endless merit in a man's knowing when to have done." I have had done with playing the cello. I have decided not to lament what I can no longer do, but to celebrate what I was allowed to do. I thank God and my teachers for this gift.

After repute, oblivion.

Marcus Aurelius

Our days are like grass,
like a field that sprouts up,
so do we blossom.

Like a wind that passes over the plant,
until it weakens and is gone,
so is the place where we stood
remembered no longer.

Psalm 103

Like the first bracing wind of winter comes this jarring—and unwelcome—word from the Roman emperor and philosopher Marcus Aurelius. There is something so organic and beautiful about the seasons of life—spring with its youth, dreams, and energy; summer with its courage and productivity; autumn with its harvesting of rewards for work accomplished; and now winter. Every season has its own cycle and bears its own fruit. What are the fruits of the wintertime of life? Some would say "none." But others would say "a great deal":

Hasidic teaching:

> *For the unlearned, old age is winter;*
>
> *for the learned, the season harvest.*

American poet Edgar Lee Masters:

And there is the silence of old age, too full of wisdom for the tongue to utter it in words intelligible to those who have not lived the great range of life.

Roman philosopher Cicero:

Intelligence, reflection, and judgment reside in old men. Age, especially an honored old age, has so great authority that this is of more value than all the pleasures of youth.

By contrast, there's Marcus Aurelius and Psalm 103. What to make of this? It seems to me that everyone is right if one understands old age in the larger context of life as a whole. Despite the emphasis of our society on youth, history teaches that there can be (and often is) great value and beauty in old age. But beauty is in the eye of the beholder.

The Japanese aesthetic concept of Wabi Sabi finds beauty in impermanence and imperfection. Terms like impermanence, humility, asymmetry, and imperfection are part of the vocabulary of this school of art and thought. Contrast this with the western concept of beauty, which prizes symmetry, grandeur, and perfection. In our society, old age, with its unavoidable signs of deterioration, is an embarrassment. The idea that oblivion might follow repute is demoralizing and frightening. When you are no longer useful to the Firm, you are ceremonially (or not so ceremonially) shuffled off the stage and quickly forgotten. In essence, exiled into oblivion, "and the place where we stood remembered no longer."

The question is, is oblivion bad? What happens when the place where I once stood remembers me no more? The answer depends on how important "repute" is to me. If it is the most important thing in my life, and defines who I am to myself, then oblivion is a kind of death—the kind where you don't physically die, but live in constant remorse of what you've lost. Unrelieved, it becomes a form of torture.

Marcus Aurelius has something to teach those of us who have tasted the humiliation of oblivion. He wants to remind us that oblivion is natural, unalterable, and an inevitable stage of life. After you step down, no matter how indispensable you were, life goes on and time erases the collective memory. It can't be any other way. If you cannot accept that truth, life will be miserable.

There is another side. If we can transcend our culturally conditioned definitions, we can move into another dimension of reality where certain truths (about ourselves, the world in which we live, and the Divine) become manifest. The great German writer Hermann Hesse described it this way:

> *Advanced age is quite necessary to experience what I have in mind; a great deal has to be seen, lived, thought through, felt, and suffered; a certain weakening of life's vital urges is necessary, as too a certain frailty and closeness to death, for one to be able, in a small manifestation, to perceive God, the essence of things, the mystery of life, the great oneness.*

"I only regret that I have but one life to lose for my country."

Nathan Hale (1776)

This was a banner day for me. For the first time in my life, I felt I was doing something patriotic for my country by playing "Taps" for the Masonic Village Memorial Day celebration.

All my life I have been unpatriotic. Patriotism was never a highly-held value in my home. Though I marched in the Los Angeles Sheriff's Boys Band as a kid on national holidays, watched the July Fourth fireworks every year from our balcony, and have watched the Memorial Day celebration on TV for years, I have never felt a personal sense of patriotism for my country.

In college, my aim was to apply for a draft deferment as a pre-med student so as not to interrupt my studies. But in my first year in Zurich, I received notice to report to Stuttgart, Germany for induction. In utter panic, I wrote Dad asking him to write his congressman to see if he could get me deferred. In the meantime, I spent three days at a U.S. Army depot in Stuttgart going through an induction physical. Soon thereafter, I received notice that my draft status was changed to allow me to finish medical school. My sense of relief was indescribable. By the time I finished medical school and residency training, I was too old for induction.

But as the years have gone on, I have felt guilty about my lack of commitment to my country. It never dawned on me that I owed my country something back for the freedom and liberty it provided me.

Fast forward to today and playing "Taps." It dawned on me that playing "Taps" is a way I can express my gratitude to my fellow countrymen and women who paid the ultimate price for the cause of freedom. There is a perpetual flame statue here on campus on which is inscribed: "All gave some, some gave all." That has always moved me. Today I was able—probably for the first time in my life—to say a heartfelt "thank you" through my trumpet. I felt humbled and cleansed.

What you are in love with,
what seizes your imagination,
will affect everything.
It will decide what will get you out of
bed in the morning,
what you will do with your evenings,
how you will spend your weekends,
what you read, what you know,
what breaks your heart,
and what amazes you with joy and gratitude.
Fall in love, stay in love, and it will decide everything.

Pedro Arrupe

Human beings who leave behind them no great
achievements, but only a sequence of small kindnesses, have
not had wasted lives.

Charlotte Gray

I long to accomplish a great and noble task.
But it is my chief duty to accomplish
humble tasks as though they were great and noble.

Helen Keller

Simon, do you really love me?

John 21:17

Last week, in our book group, we read the poem by Pedro
Arrupe. I was taken by this poem for several reasons. First, the

statement "what you are in love with" seems not to be a reference to "**Who** you are in love with," but "**What** you are in love with." That signaled a reference to something beyond a specific person (my wife, my partner, my friend, etc.), and instead to a life project that transcends my ordinary attachments, and gives my life the direction and meaning described in the heart of the poem. Second, I'm struck by the verbs he uses in describing the effect of the "what": "**Affects** everything," "**Breaks** your heart," "**Amazes** you," "**Decides** everything." Third, the phrase "fall in love, stay in love" is the language of relationship. He also makes a distinction between falling in love and staying in love. Anyone who has been in a relationship of any length knows that the two are not the same. It's easy to fall in love, but hard to stay in love after the "falling in love" phase passes. And lastly, the capacity to stay in love "will decide everything." In the end, life is not about just any kind of love, but about this kind of love.

When I think back on our group, we were impressed by the beauty and import of the poem. But none of us stated "what"—if anything—we were in love within our individual lives. I have asked myself: "What are YOU in love with?" As I thought about this, I remembered a conversation Jesus had with Peter (recorded in the 21st chapter of the Gospel of John). Jesus asked Peter if he loved Him. Peter immediately said "yes." But Jesus asked him again: "Peter, do you REALLY love me?" That verse has haunted me for sixty years because it implies a level of emotional commitment to Christ beyond intellectual agreement. Agreement with the rightness and rectitude of a cause or a person is not the same thing as love. Jesus was looking for love from Peter. He is looking for love from me.

What I am in love with, what seizes my imagination, what affects everything I do? The answer to that question has, for my entire adult life, been defined by my desire to be a competent, caring physician, and to serve God and humanity with the training and tools He gave me. Medicine has been a calling and not a business-model career choice for me. Thus, my response to the first line in Pedro Arrupe's poem is to say: serving God through medicine is what I have been in love with. It's who I am and what I do.

But times change. I no longer serve God as a physician because I am retired. This has brought me into a new and challenging stage of life. The physical and cognitive ability to function as I did is no longer available to me. The arc of biology in which I now find myself has forced me to redefine who I am and what my life project is. My response to the poem has changed. This is why the quotes from Charlotte Gray and Helen Keller are meaningful. I no longer give lectures, care for patients, sit on committees, or make "big" decisions. I now live a life of gentle repose, and am learning how to "accomplish humble tasks as though they were great and noble."

And what are those humble tasks? And with what attitude? In my heart of hearts, I want to love people the way Jesus loved people. Old age and the awkwardness imposed on me by my stroke have helped me to do this. I now have an understanding and tenderness toward older people I never had. I want to help lighten their load with a smile, a word of encouragement, or something as insignificant as helping them on with their overcoat. Kindness is the fruit of compassionate aging.

A wise person knows when and how

to make the exception of every rule.

Barry Schwartz

For the last fifty years, I have been part of a religious tradition that doesn't allow for exceptions to the rules. The rules are from God and meant to be followed. Inability to do so is a sign of moral weakness and will not be tolerated.

And yet my life experiences instruct me otherwise. There are rules, and there are principles. The two are not the same. We set down rules for our kids because their brains are not yet mature enough to handle exceptions to the rules. Poor impulse control is the hallmark of adolescence—not because the kids won't obey, but because their brains give them no choice. To protect them—and ourselves—we lay down rules that must be followed, and use punishment as the guarantor of enforcement.

But there comes a time when rules need to be replaced by principles. Rules tell us specifically what we are not allowed to do. Principles teach us the overarching reasons that inform our behavioral decisions, and leave it up to us as to how we will ethically and morally apply the principle. I tell my sixteen-year-old: "You must be home by ten o'clock." I tell my twenty-one-year-old: "Mom and Dad worry about you. If you're going to be late, please call so that we know that you're okay." One is a rule that says: "Thou shalt not." The other is a principle that says: "You must now live your life in a way that takes into consideration other people's concerns and feelings. Guide your conduct accordingly."

To allow oneself to make exceptions is tricky business in human relations. To do so cavalierly belies an immaturity that needs to break rules simply because they are there to be broken. The movement from adolescent dependence to adult independence is fraught with dangers—dangers every parent knows. But unless our kids can make that move, they never become fully adult.

It is the hallmark of wisdom to understand the complexity and nuance of human behavior. Every society has had its sages—men and women graced with the ability to see beyond the obvious, and discern when and how we ought to respond to the exigencies of the moment. We trust and revere these people because they understand the principles of human behavior so well, and understand themselves so well, that they can discern guiding principles where we can only see confusing rules. They know that there are always exceptions. More importantly, they know the impulsiveness and chicanery of the human heart, and can help us survive the turbulent waters of difficult decision-making. He who has a wise friend is blessed indeed.

I long to accomplish a great and noble task.
But it is my chief duty to accomplish
humble tasks as though they were great and noble.

Helen Keller

There is a part of me that has always wanted to be someone I am not. Not just a physician, but a great and famous physician; not just a cellist, but a gifted cellist; not just a smart guy, but a really smart guy. It's all rather adolescent, I know. In fact, I consider it a character flaw.

The ability to accept who one is, and to accept the talents and tasks one has been given is one of the hallmarks of a healthy, mature ego. Helen Keller was a woman of immense stature, and one of the great minds of the twentieth century. Ironically, even she struggled with this temptation. The disparity between one's reach and grasp is a temptation common—though not unique—to educated and successful people. In itself, this is not bad, for tenacious striving can spur one to greater accomplishments. But it has a downside. Hidden behind the desire to achieve often lies the sense of inadequacy rooted in an anxiety that began in childhood.

The ability to come to grips with who we are takes time. During the springtime of life, the call is to "accomplish great and noble tasks"—to find out who we are, stretch and be stretched, and reach our limits. It is only after midlife has been reached that we begin to see the limits of our dreams, and must figure out a way to deal with the painful disparity between who we are and who we wanted to be.

Helen Keller's way was to imbue her humble tasks with greatness so that they became meaningful and bearable. She didn't fool herself by calling little things big. On the contrary, her tasks were not as great and noble as she had apparently hoped. How she dealt with this disparity was more important. She relinquished the youthful desire for worldly greatness, and replaced it with a more mature, age-appropriate, re-definition of herself and her tasks. In other words, her attitude changed to accommodate her new circumstances. Herein lies her greatness—and the lesson for me: to see and accept reality as it is, and not try to be someone I'm not. To find value and importance in what I'm doing and, avoid the temptation to validate my self-worth by reaching further than I should.

On the path of the others are resting places,
places in the sun where they can meet.
But this is not your path,
and it is now that you must not fail.
Weep if you can, but do not complain.
The way chose you —
and you must be thankful.

Dag Hammarskjold

There is something about this aphorism that has haunted me for years. As a poet, translator, diplomat, and Secretary General of the United Nations, Dag Hammarskjold knew the burdens of physical fatigue and emotional isolation. A man of sensitivity and insight, he bore in his heart that which I bear in mine - namely, an ineffable awareness that one has to be called to walk a particular path, and that the only appropriate response is gratitude, not complaint.

For Hammarskjold, the path was that of a great statesman whom the world revered. Such a path is both a blessing and a curse. Little does the world know the price a famous person pays in order to remain faithful to their calling. The 18th-century French Divine Francois Fenelon was right when he wrote:

"God is ingenious in making us crosses... He makes them of gold and precious stones which dazzle the spectators and excite the envy of the public, but which crucify no less than crosses which are most despised. He makes them of all the things we like the best, and turns them to bitterness. Favor brings vexation and importunity. It gives what we do not want, and takes away what we should like."

The call is not to greatness, but to faithfulness. My path is vastly different from that of Dag Hammarskjold. Yet the response must be the same: awareness and gratitude. Sooner or later, everyone is called to bear the burdens of aging, illness, family unhappiness, or career disappointment. For most of us, life hasn't turned out the way we thought it would. We are who we are, and cannot escape. The task is to adjust in ways that allow us to grow and not be destroyed by the disappointments of unfulfilled dreams.

Here Hammarskjold is helpful to me because he points to a meaning and purpose beyond my pain. In granting the possibility that there is meaning beyond the absurdity of a life, I am able to avoid falling into the pit of self-pity and despair. To survive, I must own not only my pain, but also my path. To fail to do this is to give in to the temptation of allowing my pain to become transformed into suffering.

Hammarskjold knows that the pain of our circumstances is really not our suffering. Pain becomes suffering when we can find no meaning in what we are going through and can see no end to it. Once this takes hold, we have entered despair.

There is nothing harder in life than to be thankful for the difficult circumstances one faces. No matter how hard we try, we cannot intellectualize our way to gratitude. It is a gift from God. It was a gift for Hammarskjold—himself a man who held religion at a distance. But there was a day when, to his surprise, he mysteriously knew that there was a larger context to his life than he realized. Whatever that moment was, he came to know that "the Way chose you, and you must be thankful."

When Francis of Assisi kissed the leper:

"What before had been nauseating to me became sweetness and life."

There are people and situations in all our lives that make us recoil with nausea. More often than not, these situations remind us of something (or someone) so painful in our own past that we simply cannot bear that memory, and so find ways to avoid the confrontation. For Francis, it was a leper. For me, it is my cello.

I have played the cello for over fifty years. Though I do not play it well, it has been a source of joy for most of my adult life. It has been the one place I could go to escape the stress and pain of life. An hour with Bach gives me the strength and courage to bear the burdens that bog me down. But I have developed an intention tremor of my right arm that has made holding the bow almost impossible. Despite neurological consultation and numerous medications, nothing has changed. It is now painfully apparent that this is the way it is going to be. My performing days are over.

This experience has been so painful that I said to myself: "I can't bear to play anymore if I can't play well." The problem was, though, that I simply could not walk away from it. The desire to make a beautiful sound haunted me. Yet every time I tried, it sounded terrible, and created unbearable frustration and remorse. And so it remained until I read this quote from Francis of Assisi.

I have come to see that the root problem is that I can't have my way. I have spent my whole life overcoming obstacles and achieving my goals by hard work and fierce determination. But that modus operandi won't solve this problem. Like every chronic illness, it won't go away. I have tried everything, but nothing works. So now I am left with the task of figuring out how to live with what has become a fact of life for me.

This much I know: if I remain determined to reach my goal, I will wear myself out and become bitter. The bitterness that says: "How can you work so hard and lose it all?" The bitterness that says: "It isn't fair. I've worked too hard." Shock creates a certain kind of sadness that breeds anger, resentment, and self-pity. At this point, I'm stuck with an emotional illness that is greater than the original neurological disease.

There is profound wisdom and healing in being able to kiss the leper. For me, kissing the leper means saying "yes" to the very thing I detest. But how to do this? I am coming to understand what the Egyptian Nobel Laureate Naguib Mahfouz meant when he wrote: "The loss of an illusion became a source of strength."

It is an illusion to believe that I can overcome this neurological impediment. More than that, I am called to see that this loss can be an invitation to a new way of understanding myself and God's working in my life. I am at a time in life where getting to do what I want can no longer be the central driving force of my existence. I must learn how to "let go" in order to achieve other, more important goals. It is the God knows something I don't know—namely, the only way I will be free from the tyranny of perfection is to kiss the leper. The moment I do, the nausea will become "sweetness and life."

The harp that once through Tara's halls
the soul of music shed, now hangs as mute
on Tara's walls as if that soul were fled. -
So sleeps the pride of former days,
so glory's thrill is o'er, and hearts,
that once beat high for praise,
now feel that pulse no more.

Thomas Moore (1779-1852)

Last evening, I had dinner with a small group of friends—men whose company I enjoy immensely. We had a delightful evening, relishing good food, good wine, good music, and good conversation. Soon the mood turned to politics and the plight of our country. Everyone had an opinion on what has gone wrong, and how the ship of state ought to be made to run better. Everyone except me. I listened intently to all the opinions, but offered none of my own. Sitting there, I thought of the Indian saying: "Before speaking, consider if it is an improvement on silence." I decided that it wasn't. The evening drew to a close, and we parted with gratitude for having been together. On the way home, I wondered why I had not participated in the political discussion. After all, I am an active member of the group and have opinions about other things that I share without hesitation. Why did I become silent?

Looking back, I remember feeling quietly detached from the discussion. It was not that I was disinterested in what was said. It was more of a kind of benevolent detachment from their concerns. I've noticed that about myself recently. Issues and concerns that once stirred me to the core—e.g., medical care, societal violence, international conflicts—no longer do so. It is as if my world of civic concern is shrinking. I find myself content to live with the ambiguity and turbulence of the world

66

around me without the need to fix it. It is almost as if a veil separates me from the world. It is not that I don't care. I follow the news as carefully as I ever did. Rather, my focus of concern has moved beyond the exigencies of the moment to a context that is both larger and more personal.

There comes a time in every man's life when the focus of attention changes. The need to be vitally informed, to hold strong opinions, and take immediate action has now passed for me. The pride of former days, the addictive need for glory, the heart that once beat for praise, is dying a good death. This is why I think I sat quietly last evening enjoying the conversation without feeling a compulsive need to participate. I was content to be lovingly present to my friends in silence.

The best mirror is an old friend.

George Herbert

The older I grow, the more I realize the importance—more than that, the necessity—of a certain kind of friend. What I have in mind is a friend who is not only comfortable and amiable, but trustworthy, discerning, and courageous. These are rare qualities—certainly in our age, but probably in any age—and form the foundation for what I think George Herbert meant by "an old friend."

An old friend has usually walked with us a long time, knows our strengths and weaknesses, and has gained our trust. However, longevity of relationship has little to do with discernment and courage. And it is just these two qualities that are so important in the development of true friendship.

Friendship is the highest form of human love. The greatest loves portrayed in poetry and literature—whether they were consummated in marital love or not—have always been founded on a partnership of the soul. Why is this? It is because the friend (who in a profound way becomes a partner) loves not only the mind but also the soul of the other. This is what Victor Hugo meant when, in **Les Misérables**, he wrote: "To love another person is to see the face of God." We see the face of God when we give ourselves to our partner in ways that allow his/her soul to grow.

What I have in mind is the willingness to allow my friend to hold a mirror up to my face so that I might see things s/he can see, but I can't. To do this requires insight, courage, receptivity, and humility. We all have "blind spots"—that is, psychological defense mechanisms (almost always dating back to childhood) that remain unconscious, and thus inaccessible. These "blind spots" influence how we respond to certain situations in our everyday lives and create difficulties in our relationships. The tragedy is that we will remain oblivious to these deficits and continue to make the same mistakes until someone points them out. It is here that a true friend can help us—if s/he has discernment, courage, and wisdom.

In order to do this, one has to be willing to relinquish the typical American idea of independence and move toward an attitude of interdependence. The best examples I can think of are found in music, sports, and surgery. As disparate as these disciplines are, they have this in common: every great singer has a coach to whom s/he regularly goes to work out technical difficulties in delivery and phrasing; every great baseball pitcher has a pitching coach to whom he regularly turns for problems in delivery; and every accomplished surgeon, when he encounters an insurmountable intra-operative problem, will ask a respected colleague to "scrub in" for assistance.

All this is based on the awareness that I cannot master "the task" by myself, that a trusted expert can see things I cannot see, and that if I can submit to the authority of "my friend," I will be better off. But here is the rub: it's all about humility. That is, my willingness to accept the reality of unperceived deficits within myself, and that I need outside input in order to improve. Until this is appreciated and accepted, nothing will change, and "the mirror" will be seen as an enemy and not a friend.

I have a friend who recently held a mirror up to my face; it was not pretty, and my predictable response was anger and denial. After a few days, I wrote her and said: "Thank you for helping me face my fears, my pride, and my pettiness." That incident reminded me of just how dependent we are on one another for our growth, and how vital it is to have friendships capable of mirroring and being mirrored. By that I mean, mirroring in true friendships works both ways. As we grow in love and trust, we open ourselves up in ways that allow the mirroring to take place in both directions. My friend wrote back: "Please do the same for me." There is nothing more important than having "an old friend."

Only those who are themselves in need of
being treated kindly can be gentle and
forbearing with others.

Hermann Hesse

For the last week, I have been plagued by a viral bronchitis—the kind that makes you cough day and night, spew purulent material from your nose and mouth, wet your pants, and makes life miserable. This afternoon, just before going to visit my wife in the nursing home, I noticed some purulent material on my sweater—the product of a violent coughing spell that exploded before I could find a Kleenex. As I stood looking at the mess on my sweater, I thought how helpless we are at certain moments in life, and how very human this incident is.

An hour later, sitting across from Betty in the nursing home, she dropped food from her mouth without realizing it. As the cream pudding slowly slid down onto her bib without her realizing it, I suddenly saw myself standing in front of the bathroom mirror gazing with disgust at the mess on my sweater. And then I knew the wisdom of Hermann Hesse's saying.

I don't think anyone can be gentle and forbearing unless they have been touched by their own weakness and need for kindness. There is something emotionally detached about "feeling sorry for" another person in distress. Sympathy is good, but insufficient. It's insufficient because it emanates from a "noblesse oblige" position of moral superiority. That is, I'm not like you, but I will help you. There is value in this, to be sure. But, as Hesse says, the proffered charity will lack gentleness and forbearance because one has not walked in the shoes of the other. To know pain, fear, humiliation,

71

helplessness, and hopelessness is to know how life-giving gentleness and forbearance can be. These are qualities that cannot be dispensed like good advice. They can only come from a painful place within the person who has been there.

As I sat there watching the pudding drool down her face onto her lap, I understood—probably for the first time—that wonderful German word "*Mitgefuhl.*" It is a word I learned years ago (and thought I understood) while studying in Zurich. It means "feeling with," and is a seldom-used, intimate expression of identification with the pain of the other. I knew the word intellectually. But today I knew it emotionally. To "feel with" another is to have been touched by the same pain as the other. The "*mit*" ("with") of the word implies a deep personal identification with the suffering of the other. Short of that, one is expressing sympathy, but not *Mitgefuhl*. Betty's shame and embarrassment today was my own shame and embarrassment earlier in the day. Without realizing it, there came pouring forth from me a gentleness and forbearance devoid of judgment, criticism, or embarrassment. This is who we all are: people in need of being treated kindly.

As we grow older the world becomes stranger,
the pattern more complicated
of dead and living.

T.S. Eliot: Four Quartets

They are strangers in the world as I am.

Jesus: John 17:16

Something is happening to me. I have become a stranger in my own home. The things I used to enjoy, the company I used to keep, the food I used to relish—all this is now only relatively important. To be sure, there are a few friends whose company I cherish. But the list has dwindled—not so much because they have died or moved away, but because I no longer have anything to say to them. This sounds like a portrait of a depressed person. But I'm not. On the contrary, I'm more alive than I have ever been. It's just that I have changed. I am not who I was.

Yesterday I made a list of things I need in my life:

1. the love and companionship of a few friends

2. meaning and purpose in my work

3. solitude

4. my books

5. music

6. warmth

7. a comfortable bed

8. a faith sufficient to sustain me in the valley of darkness and death

What strikes me about this list is what is NOT included: health, worldly success, financial security, popularity, and a reforming zeal for social justice. Health is a gift to be cherished. But the world is filled with people who do not have health and yet live rich and fulfilled lives. I conclude that health is a gift and highly prized, but not essential to a life well lived. Worldly success, financial security, and popularity are likewise not essential to a fruitful life. To be sure, they make life easier and sometimes more enjoyable (poverty is itself not a virtue). But the danger of addiction to success, wealth, and popularity is so great that the burden ultimately outweighs the benefit. Even the zeal for social justice—itself noble—becomes tempered over time. Maybe that is because the older one grows, the more one's energy diminishes. And with that diminishment comes a narrowing of vision for what can be accomplished. This is why the old need to make way for the young. Although the younger generation lacks our experience and wisdom, they are not jaded by our disappointments and cynicism. Their naïveté, enthusiasm, creativity, and strength meet challenges beyond our scope.

I am beginning to realize that growing old, if it is to be fruitful, requires a kind of disengagement from the world. By "disengagement," I do not mean "isolation." I mean a shift in attention from external reality to internal reality. In the first half of life, the external world is the only world one knows. Life is defined by the goals and aspirations one establishes for himself: education, career development, marriage, family, and community service. This is as it should be. In fact, if these goals are not met, one cannot successfully move on to the second half of life where the goals, methods, and accomplishments are completely different. Intense engagement with the world is the agenda for the first half of life. Intense disengagement is the goal of the second half of life.

To grow old is a painful and often disorienting experience in our culture. Contemporary norms and values, with their preferential bias toward youth, make it impossible to transition from "young" to "old" with ease, confidence, and equanimity. In a society in which aging is synonymous with decline, deterioration, and death, it is well-nigh impossible to imagine that anyone on Medicare could have something valuable to say. How vastly different it is in other cultures where age is venerated and wisdom is prized.

What is it about becoming a stranger that makes Eliot say what he did? A few verses down, he gives us the answer:

"Old men ought to be explorers. Here and there does not matter. We must be still and still moving into another intensity for a further union, a deeper communion... In my end is my beginning."

Here we have it: "another intensity, a further union, a deeper communion." Eliot is declaring that there is more to life than what is possible—and even imaginable—in the first half of life. To be sure, education, success, and wealth are necessary to achieve the goals of the first half of life. But they are insufficient for the work in the second half of life. How utterly bizarre that there is something beyond fame, fortune, and good health! Isn't hard work and success enough? That's what I was taught and believed. But it isn't so. There is a whole new world to be experienced this side of death—a world of values and perspective vastly different from the one-dimensional world I grew up striving to become a part of.

To be old and be an explorer, to be still and still moving into another intensity—this is Eliot's goal. But this is only possible if one can launch out into the unchartered waters of inner growth. If one can do this, Eliot predicts, one will discover that "in my end is my beginning."

If one pursues this path, as Jesus predicts, one will become a stranger in the world. There is something about changing your outlook on life that alienates you from family and friends. New ways of thinking always upset the apple cart, create dissension and social isolation. Eventually, there is nothing more to talk about. That was true for Jesus, and is true for every person who gets a glimpse of "a further union, a deeper communion."

Maybe this separation of age is what Edgar Lee Masters had in mind when he wrote:

> *There is the silence of age,*
> *Too full of wisdom for the tongue to*
> *utter it*
> *In words intelligible to those who have*
> *not lived*
> *The great range of life.*

Long years must pass before the truths
we have made for ourselves
become our flesh.

Paul Valery

The nineteenth-century French poet Paul Valery knew something I never knew—namely, it takes years before a foundational truth becomes part of our being. I stand amazed at the number of "truths" I have discovered over the years that simply remained intellectual insights without ever becoming part of my operational life. When I look at texts, I have underlined or notes and dates I have penned in the margins, I am struck by two things: first, how correct my notes were and second, how far back some of those dates go. It's like I saw these truths way back then, but somehow they remained frozen as intellectual insights without ever having affected my life. In other words, the insights stayed in my head but never moved down to my heart.

Growth and development are incremental. Those longed-for sudden insights, flashes of enlightenment, mountain-top experiences, and Eureka moments are to be treasured, but need to be worked out over time in the nitty-gritty of our daily lives. Or, as Paul Valery would say: "... become our flesh."

What does "become our flesh" mean? It means moving an idea from the left hemisphere of the brain (where conscious, rational thinking takes place) to deeper, integrated parts of the brain where the "insight" is transformed into a pattern of thinking and behavior that is now unconscious—a part of who we are. This transformational movement does not happen overnight. In fact, it happens slowly—as does all biological maturation.

When I look back over the liner notes I have made over the years, I am dismayed at the little progress in character formation I have made. My discouragement is understandable. But it is also delusional. All growth—physical, intellectual, emotional, spiritual—is a lifelong process for which there is no well-defined end point. Valery says "Long years..." But I want it now...

Our judgments judge us, and nothing reveals us or exposes
our weaknesses more ingeniously than an attitude of
pronouncing upon our fellows.

Paul Valery

Make no judgments where you have no compassion.

Anne McCaffrey

There is a principle that cannot fail to keep a man in
everlasting ignorance. That principle is "contempt prior to
investigating."

Herbert Spencer

Do not judge by appearances,

but judge with right judgment.

John 7:24

Life is about making judgments. We do it dozens of times a day—from trivial and daily to momentous and life-changing. In fact, the hallmark of maturity is the capacity to make reasoned judgments for ourselves, our families, our community, and our nation. Decision-making is the way we go through life.

An esteemed ethicist once said: "We all do ethics. The question is: do we all do good ethics?" The same can be said about making judgments. Some do it better than others. If this is true, then it is the responsibility of each of us to examine ourselves to see if we can do a better job.

Each of these quotes points out a pitfall in the process of making judgments.

Paul Valery points out the danger of "pronouncing" on our fellows. His use of the word "pronouncing" suggests a pejorative attitude toward the person being judged. His point is, when we "pronounce," we are advertising our own bias and weakness of character. More often than not, the intensity of our voice, the choice of our words, and body posture advertise an inner conflict we harbor that says more about us than it does about the issue at hand.

Anne McCaffrey takes Valery's argument to its logical conclusion by declaring that where there is no compassion—that is, where what we are doing is "pronouncing"—then we should exempt ourselves from making a judgment. If that were the case, I suspect that most of the judgments we make would have to be deferred for lack of compassion on the part of the decision-maker.

Herbert Spencer's observation is as relevant today as it was in the nineteenth century—namely, the temptation to pass judgment before fully assessing the data. It's all about bias and preconceptions we bear regarding certain people(s), circumstances, and ways of life which we abhor. There is always an unconscious "contempt" hidden beneath the surface which flavors, informs, and directs our thinking about the person or cause in question. Until I face my (often hidden) contempt, Spencer suggests that I will remain locked in my own ignorance.

And finally, Jesus warns against what probably is the commonest cause of poor decision-making—namely, settling for surface assessment. Everyone is prone to this. Yet superficiality can be deadly—as our legal system bears witness to in the number of innocent men and women who spend years behind bars.

Pronouncing, lack of compassion, contempt prior to investigation, and superficiality. All of these are issues of attitude and have little to do with the externals of judgment. Facts alone don't constitute truth. Truth takes the facts and places them in the larger context of lived life, and arrives at a multi-layered understanding of right judgment. This is called wisdom.

War never determines who's right - just who's left.

Bertrand Russell

All history is little more than a long succession

of useless cruelties.

Voltaire

No battle is ever won. They are not even fought. The field only reveals to man his folly and despair, and victory is an illusion of philosophers and fools.

William Faulkner

War is the unfolding of miscalculations.

Barbara Tuchman

What we have learned from history is that we haven't learned from history.

Benjamin Disraeli

The older I grow, the more disturbed I have become about the endless number of wars there are in this world. I grew up with WW II and Korea. Then there was Vietnam. And now Iraq, Afghanistan, and Syria—to say nothing of Israel, Palestine, Iran, Yemen, Egypt, Ukraine, Russia, ISIS. The list goes on. There is no end to it. And probably never will be. And that's the rub: there doesn't appear to be a way out of armed conflict in solving international problems.

From my tiny vantage point on the periphery of world affairs, I see no way out—except for the absolute conviction that war is not the answer. I am theologically not an Anabaptist only because I am sadly persuaded that there are international conflicts that require armed intervention—e.g., ISIS. I see no way here out of the need to meet their irrationality and brutality other than with aggressive intervention. Diplomacy has failed because they are incapable of being reasoned with. Peace can only come on their terms. At the same time, I recoil at the thought of what this will mean. Miscalculation on one side inevitably leads to miscalculation on the other side until blood is everywhere. Have we not learned that from Iraq and Afghanistan?

This problem is not new. It is as old as civilization. There is something inside man that wants (or needs) to conquer his neighbor. This reminds me of the Garden of Eden story of man desiring the apple, biting into it, and then blaming the woman for his action. We seem never to be satisfied with what we have. We possess an insatiable desire to take what doesn't belong to us, and an uncanny ability to concoct sophisticated strategies to justify that desire. And it always seems right in our eyes. I'm almost driven to agree with the prophet Jeremiah: "The heart is deceitful above all things, and desperately corrupt; who can understand it?"

When you choose an action,

you choose the consequences of that action.
Anon.

I wish someone had told me that when I was young. It might have tempered some of the stupid things I did—or wanted to do but couldn't. On the other hand, maybe not. Passion and determination—not forethought and the capacity for delayed gratification—are the hallmarks of youth. Even if I had considered the possible outcomes of my decisions, I might have charged ahead, anyway. Probably so.

But now things look different. With the dispassionate clarity of old age, I see how important it is to consider the consequences of an action before undertaking that action. The English essayist Robert Louis Stevenson once said: "Everybody, sooner or later, sits down to a banquet of consequences."

On the other hand, there are difficulties with such an admonition. The first is the universal veil of ignorance common to adolescence and young adulthood. Under ordinary circumstances, it is not possible for a young person to "choose" the consequences of an action. For a young person, life experience is so limited, passion so intense, and the amygdala/prefrontal cortex pathways of the brain so undeveloped that it is simply not possible to self-correct in those moments when desire exceeds discretion. The ability to temper intense desires with sober reflection comes with time and brain maturation—and for some, not even then. The second difficulty is the difficulty in accurately discerning the consequences of actions even for the wise. While it is true that we think about life retrospectively, the truth is that we live life prospectively. Many (if not most) of our decisions are made under the constraints of time pressure, insufficient data, and not knowing exactly what the consequences will be.

And yet there is wisdom in this aphorism. It is true that youth must live with the painful consequences of wrong decisions. It is also true that we cannot always foresee the outcomes of our decisions. Nevertheless, it is critically important to hold this aphorism in mind to give me pause in my sometimes biased and all-too-quick-and-automatic decision-making process. If I don't, my "banquet of consequences" will be larger than it already is.

This is the greatest skill of all,

to take the bitter with the sweet

and make it beautiful,

to take the whole of life in all its moods,

its strengths and weaknesses,

and of the whole make one great and celestial harmony.

Robert Terry Weston

It has been one year since Betty died. One year in grieving the loss of my partner; one year in learning how to be a widower; one year in learning how to start a new chapter of life. What have I learned? It seems at times not much. The intense grief has mercifully faded into the background so that I am able to connect with the world without distress. I can laugh again, and I don't feel as bereft as I did. Much—if not all—of this is due to my closest friends, who have borne me up on the wings of their love, patience, and kindness. Without them, I should have perished.

Perhaps the most important lesson I am learning is how to acknowledge, appreciate, and be comfortable with the duality of bitter and sweet in forming a full and meaningful life. This, as Robert Terry Weston writes, is the greatest skill of all. Just as learning how to strive and achieve is the goal that brings the sweet trophies to the first half of life, so learning how to let go of those very trophies is the great task of the second half of life, and essential for survival in the winter season of life.

Slowly I am learning that this task cannot be accomplished until one has first lost those very things necessary for a meaningful first half of life: energy, health, youth, success, reputation. C.G. Jung once said:

We cannot live the afternoon of life according to the program of life's morning. What was great in the morning will be little in the evening, and what in the morning was true will at evening become a lie.

Here is the truth: morning without evening risks pain and bitterness because it lacks a larger context of meaning and strength to survive the losses of inevitable deterioration. Evening without morning risks the bitterness and cynicism that comes when one has no memories of youth, young love, challenges met, or hard-won battles fought. The two belong together like two sides of a coin. And the result: a wholeness of being that can lovingly accommodate "the whole of life in all its moods, its strengths and weaknesses."

The wise man forgets insults
as the ungrateful forget benefits.

Chinese proverb

The art of being wise is the art of knowing what to overlook.

William James

To become wise is the great task of the second half of life. That much is clear to me. What is not clear is how to obtain wisdom, and what wisdom looks like in practical terms. It's one thing to opine on the subject of wisdom, but another to be a wise man.

There is a vast literature on the subject of wisdom in both eastern and western societies. What has impressed me is the remarkable agreement on the characteristics of a wise person. Invariably these are the qualities most esteemed: patience, tolerance, prudence in speech, caution in making decisions, awareness of one's limitations, gentleness in correcting others, discretion in keeping secrets, the ability to see the larger picture in human interactions, a willingness to forgive, and the capacity to give others the benefit of the doubt. These traits make one wise, respected, and trustworthy.

The art of knowing what to overlook is clearly one of the most important tasks in life. Absent that, life becomes unmanageable because everything takes on the same level of importance. I want to apply this definition of wisdom to human relationships. I think the Chinese admonition to "forget" means the same as James' admonition "to overlook." To overlook a hurt or forget an insult is hard for me to do. It is clear that there are things one cannot overlook—issues so paramount to the integrity of the relationship that they must be dealt with. But that's not what I am thinking of. I'm thinking of the minor wounds of misunderstanding and miscommunication that make up so much of our daily life at home or at work. When these little wounds fester, irritation grows into insult, and resentment takes hold. Resentment left unchecked, poisons the best of relationships.

How to forget insults and knowing what to overlook is an unsolved mystery that has haunted man from time immemorial. It is therefore not surprising that neither the Chinese nor William James have the answer. It is perhaps enough for today that I am able to recognize that I don't have the answer, either. On the other hand, facing this disparity in my own life and humbly seeking a solution is perhaps a small step in becoming a wise man.

Be constantly reminded to respect

and obey the powers that be,

to speak ill of no one, to avoid quarreling, to be forbearing,

and under all circumstances to show

a gentle spirit in dealing with others,

whoever they may be.

Titus 3:1-3

There is, however, a limit at which forbearance ceases to be a virtue.

Edmund Burke

To forbear means "to refrain, to tolerate, to endure." This is a noble trait. But, like all noble traits, it is impossible to realize with any sense of consistency. It is perhaps enough to earnestly desire, and strive for, attainment. But Edmund Burke, the great eighteenth-century English statesman, raises a different, and more unsettling, concern. He argues that there comes a time when forbearance ceases to be a virtue. I take this to mean that there are circumstances, in the affairs of men and nations, when forbearance no longer serves a constructive purpose and thus loses its moral imperative.

This is strong talk, and could easily be dismissed as the cant of an irreverent man. But Burke was not an irreverent man. It was he who said: "Man is by his constitution a religious animal; atheism is against not only our reason, but our instincts." In this, Burke affirmed the importance of God in the life of the individual and the State. Yet he saw forbearance as a relative and not an absolute good.

History is replete with examples of individuals (and whole communities) that chose forbearance in the face of severe injustice, and suffered the gravest of consequences. Many were religious communities that saw endurance as God's will and suffered the consequences willingly. Burke would argue that while that may be the right choice for some, it will not be for others. For those who do not choose the path of forbearance (because they are no longer able or willing), there will be no relief save through their own devices (e.g., insurrection) or through the intervention of the State which is called to protect its people whenever and wherever it can. Absent that mandate, the State has no moral legitimacy.

All this raises the question of scriptural interpretation. Taken on its face, the admonition given in Titus 3:1-3 is the essence of commonsense and civility. To speak ill of no one strikes at the heart of gossip; to avoid quarreling is the only way to deal with contentious people who want to argue for the sake of arguing; to show a gentle spirit is the only way one can have a civil society; and to be patient and forbearing with others is the heart of any meaningful relationship. So what's the problem?

I think the issue has to do with the difference between "rules" and "principles." Much of what the Bible teaches—particularly in human relations—has to do with guiding principles of behavior. Society cannot exist without agreed-on principles of conduct—principles like those outlined in Titus. Absent these, anarchy rules and society disintegrates. This much is clear. What is not so clear is the difference between rules and principles. Rules cannot be broken without the sanctioned threat of punishment (as when the parent says to the teenager leaving on a date: "I want you home by ten o'clock"). Principles, by contrast, are guidelines of conduct that require a deeper level of understanding because inherent in the principle is the possibility that an exception can be made. We are not to murder. Yet we go to war to kill. We are to honor our parents. Yet there are parents who have been so abusive that it is impossible to honor them. Some people suffer so greatly in a relationship that they can no longer endure and must find a way to escape the burden.

Life is infinitely more complicated and nuanced than most of us would like to believe. And it is getting more complicated all the time. This is forcing us to re-think the simple axioms we were raised with. Lincoln's words are again prescient:

"The dogmas of the quiet past are inadequate to the stormy present. The occasion is piled high with difficulty and we must rise to the occasion. As our case is new, so we must think anew and act anew."

The mandate to commit to principles such as those in Titus remains unchanged. But Burke offers a reminder that justice must be factored into our behavior in ways that make life bearable and harmonious. He would certainly agree with the Old Testament prophet Micah:

What does the Lord require of you

but to do justice, to love kindness,

and to walk humbly with your God?

This body is my house - it is not I;

triumphant in this faith I live and die.

Frederic Lawrence Knowles

Last evening I watched a documentary on Tibet entitled "The Snow Lion." It was a documentary on the takeover of Tibet by the Chinese government, and destruction of the Tibetan culture and religion. At the heart of the genocide of this noble culture lay the accurate assessment that the foundation of the Tibetan culture is their religion. To be a Tibetan is to be religious; to be religious is to be a Tibetan. The two are not only closely linked, but coterminous. They are fused. Thus, if you can destroy the religion, you can destroy the people. And that is just what the Communists have done. By destroying their temples and academies, and by forcing the Dalai Lama into exile, they have de facto destroyed their religion and robbed the Tibetans of their religious and social identity.

I walked away shaken at what I saw: men and women ready to die for their country and their religious heritage. These were people who would rather die than live without their faith. I thought of Nathan Hale's famous statement before his execution in 1776:

I only regret that I have but one life to lose for my country.

I wonder what I would do. Is there anything I would die for? My country, my family, my friends, my religious faith? It is the kind of question one usually does not have to answer—at least not in this country—unless one is an enlisted soldier headed for Iraq or Afghanistan. I have met a number of these men and women who have willingly and purposefully put their lives on the line for their country. And our WWII veterans? Before all these, I stand in admiration and awe.

When I was young, I had no intention of serving in the military. I wanted to be a doctor, and so used the deferment system to avoid the draft. I was grateful for this option, but have always felt guilty about not having served. Truth to tell, I have envisioned service to my country rather through medicine than military activity.

Would I be willing to die for my faith? The noble, romantic part of me says 'Yes.' Yet I know myself well enough to know that might not be true. I know also the misplaced zeal of Peter, who proudly told Jesus that he was ready to die for him—only to have Jesus predict that before morning Peter would deny him. And he did. He did so because he did not know himself, his pride, his fears, and his lack of courage. I am in touch (albeit dimly) with my vanity, my romantic zeal mixed with hubris, and my well-known history of having failed the Lord so many times already in smaller things. I would like to say 'yes', but fear I will not have the strength and courage to pay the ultimate price. I am ashamed of this, but know it to be true. I know also that it will require the grace of God to set me free to follow my Lord where and when He calls. I pray for mercy.

Be still before the Lord

and wait in patience.

... Do not fret, it only leads to evil.

Psalm 37:7

I've been struggling with a viral bronchitis for a week now. All I do is cough—day and night—with no end in sight. I'm sick of all this and want to be free from it. I have appointments scheduled and a big trip planned.

While I was sitting in my chair this evening listening to Beethoven's Opus 131 string quartet, I suddenly thought of this verse in Psalm 37. The call is not just to wait, but to wait patiently. Further, fretting doesn't help, but only makes things worse. Truth to tell, I don't know how to wait patiently. I can wait if I must (as in the checkout line at the supermarket), and that only up to a point. After that I begin fretting which leads to anxiety, anger, and sometimes saying things I will later regret.

To wait patiently is to relax in the midst of chaos and frustration. It sounds counter-intuitive, I know. The natural reaction is to react when a threshold of tolerance has been reached. I travel in a circle of friends (most of whom are highly educated and goal-oriented) who have a low frustration threshold. And I have become one of them. But the truth is, that is simply a learned phenomenon. Patience can be developed. I just don't know how.

My bronchitis is a case in point. Regardless of what I do, it will run its course—7-14 days of coughing and malaise. The usual OTC remedies may help, but probably not much. This disease has claimed me, and won't let go until it's finished. My time-honored response is disdain, frustration, and anger. In other words, "fretting." As I sat pondering this, it was like a voice that said to me: "Relax. You're here. Let it take you where it wants to go. Your job is to wait patiently." But I don't know how to wait patiently. I can wait for a while. But after that I have things to do.

I think the Ancients knew how to wait patiently. Maybe it's because they had no choice. Life then was so brutal, and the options so limited, that waiting is all they could do. I have a painting hanging on my wall a country doctor sitting beside a makeshift bed attending a sick child. The parents are distraught, the child is sick, and he has done everything he can. Now he must wait to see what the outcome will be. There is a certain calm in his face—maybe resignation—as he waits. He has been through this so many times. Through it all, he has learned to wait quietly. I have not yet learned that—at least not with myself.

To be still before the Lord is to learn patience. In Hollywood, the skies open, the music crescendos, and the hero triumphs. Not so in real life. In the real world, after you wait, there is nothing but silence. No bells, no harps, no clear answers—just silence and continued suffering. And then the answer comes: "Be still, wait patiently, don't fret." I don't want to wait any longer. I've waited long enough. I'm exhausted from coughing and sleep deprivation. But Beethoven says: "Just be quiet and listen. If you do, you will hear something from deep within."

At the end of his last Quartet (Opus 135) Beethoven wrote: "Muss es sein? Es muss sein" ("Must it be? It must be"). This deep sense of cosmic inevitability, the realization that we don't control our fate, and that things are as they are permeated his thinking, much as it permeated Rembrandt's thinking in his last self-portrait in 1669. In that painting there is a quiet—almost resigned—repose. His was the face of a man who had been through so much. Everything had been stripped from him—all the grandeur, all the hubris of success and happiness. What remained was inner composure. No more fretting, no more impatience. Just quietly, patiently waiting. Not knowing. Waiting.

To love someone is to reveal to them that they are beautiful.

Jean Vanier

It seems to me that this is the sum and substance of what a loving relationship is all about. And not just a romantic relationship, but any meaningful relationship. I think here of a child-parent relationship, a therapeutic relationship, a spiritual relationship. Any relationship of depth which has more than an immediate, consumer-oriented goal.

Inherent in this admonition is a call (as in the instance of the therapeutic encounter) to redefine what is meant by 'help' and 'beauty.' To help another is to attempt to solve a particular problem the other person brings to you. It is what I do as a physician when I prescribe a course of treatment for a patient with a particular medical problem I know how to fix. That is as it should be. But what if the problem is that the other person thinks they are ugly, unlovable, unworthy of esteem, riddled with profound personal deficits? What then?

Jean Vanier suggests that love—of a certain kind—is the only medicine that can heal. What does he mean? I think he means that love is the only tonic that can heal the soul. The kind of love that sees reality for what it is, and also the goodness and value hidden behind the immediate defeat and flaws of the other person. The wounded person cannot see her beauty. She can only see the ugliness of defeat and failure. It is the helper who must reveal to her the beauty that lies dormant in her soul. Only if the relationship grows can she trust her helper to believe what he knows to be true—namely, there is inner beauty hidden beneath the outer ugliness, and that it is possible for that beauty to emerge and become the dominant theme of her self-identity. With this new, emerging awareness, she can reverse her self-destructive attitude and become a new person.

I think beauty lies at the heart of all meaningful relationships. Sooner or later (usually sooner than later) the blush of romanticism fades as the two people get to know each other. Their differences in personality, cultural upbringing, lifestyle habits, problem-solving and child-raising skills, etc. all challenge the integrity of the commitment to a degree that one begins to wonder if maybe a mistake was made in signing on to this journey together. At the heart of all these differences is a deep (but often unrecognized) need to be understood and affirmed as the good person that one believes oneself to be. That affirmation can only come from the partner. When I am hurting, I am at my ugliest. And when I am at my ugliest, I hate myself the most and I know that I am a total failure as a partner, parent, lover, or friend. Paradoxically, it is at that moment that I need to hear your words of healing—words that can give me hope that I am not hopelessly beyond redemption.

It is no trick to tell someone that they are beautiful when all is well. Anyone can do that. The art of love lies in finding a way to "reveal to them that they are beautiful" when you (and they) do not think that they are beautiful. This is not easy. It is, in fact, the most difficult task in a relationship.

There are plenty of self-help books out there that purport to help solve the problem. I believe the key lies in the heartfelt desire and ability of each partner to reveal the beauty that lies in their heart and soul of their mate. This revelation is not a magic wand that immediately solves all problems. But that's the point. Life is not about fixing problems, but rather about revealing to each other that we are lovable, worthy human beings. If that sounds trite and even sophomoric, we need to be reminded that insecurity rooted in poor self-esteem is the single greatest problem in human relationships. Despite the bravado of youth, allure, and success, we fear that "you're okay, but I'm really not okay." The trouble is, over time, that fear can become a self-fulfilling prophecy.

Hidden in every experience is a gift.

Marcia Prager

Who is this lady who can say something as grandiose as that? Clearly she hasn't gone through enough pain. Well, I was wrong. A rabbi who has gone through a divorce, Rabbi Prager has earned the right to her opinion.

Once I began to take her seriously, I found myself wondering if her opinion squares with my experience. There was a time when pronouncements like that had the ring of ultimate truth for me. I assumed they were true, and I needed to adjust my thinking accordingly. I no longer believe that. It is incumbent on me to test a generalized statement like this against my own experience to see if there is congruity. If so, I need to accept it. If not, I need to reject it regardless of how reasonable or noble it sounds.

When I look back on my life, I can see that the doors that closed against my will were ultimately in my best interest—though at the time I was heartbroken. As is true for many, my journey has consisted of closed doors that forced me down new, and ultimately more fruitful, paths.

But not everything. There are experiences—like death, disability, and poverty—wherein there is no gift to discover. Only suffering that doesn't seem to end. This is the mystery, isn't it? To be trapped in a life situation for which there is no explanation (bad luck, bad genes, bad karma) is to be confronted not with a problem to be solved, but a mystery to be lived.

So much of life is enshrouded in mystery. Things inexplicably happen and leave nothing but devastation in their wake.

Looking for answers, one is left with conclusions like "I'll never understand," or "it must be God's will," or "it must be God's punishment," or "God means this for my own good," or, as Rabbi Prager suggests: "there is a gift hidden in this experience. You just have to dig deeper to find it." I have been looking for the gift hidden in Betty's dementia for twenty years and haven't found it. Nor has she.

At the end of it all, I don't know what to make of Rabbi Prager's statement. It is clear that always getting my way in life would have been a disaster. If I take that on faith, and if I believe in a benevolent force guiding my destiny, then the pains of disappointment and loss are bearable. But there are other momentous things that happen in life—both individually and collectively—that defy the wisdom of goodness and grace. Here faith reaches the water's edge, and one is left with the mystery of absurdity. On the other hand, maybe the Jewish mystic Abraham Joshua Heschel was right when he wrote: "There is meaning beyond the absurd." I don't know.

There is endless merit in a man's knowing

when to have done.

Thomas Carlyle

It has taken me a lifetime to grasp the importance of Carlyle's admonition. The ability to know when to walk away from a relationship, a job, or any other commitment is one of the hallmarks of true wisdom. But it is a virtue hard to come by, and almost impossible if you have been trained to hang in there at all costs. The tragedy is that if you stay in too long, the cost will be too high.

This aphorism, like so many, is more complicated than it appears. "Knowing when to have done" requires a degree of self-insight and objectivity that few of us have in the first half of life. And it is in the first half of life that most relationship and career decisions are made. For that, we are forced to depend on what we learned at home or picked up along the way. Sometimes those skills are adequate—often not. Add to that one's personality style and level of intellectual and emotional maturity, and the task can be daunting.

I was taught to prize hard work and perseverance. I still do. But I have come to realize that when these virtues become the dominant force in my work, they can overrule other, equally important, factors and create an imbalance that threatens the rest of my life. It is a truism that any virtue becomes a liability when it is overdone. The problem is that often I don't recognize when these virtues are overworked because they are part of who I am. And even if someone points it out to me, I may not be able to change. The ability to change is rare, especially in the second half of life.

Yet perseverance, when driven beyond measure, can kill. What started out as 'stubborn' eventually becomes legitimized—even ennobled—in the motto "We shall prevail." That, too, has its place. Not a few battles have been fought and won because someone determined to stay the course, and prevailed. But mottos, like aphorisms, must be judged by the situation in which we find ourselves. We need the courage to look inside, ask what purpose our perseverance serves, and have the courage to "have done" if we cannot come up with a good answer.

How many things by season season'd

are to their right praise

and true perfection!

William Shakespeare

For everything there is a season, and a time for every matter under heaven.

Ecclesiastes 3:1

Life, like nature, has four seasons: spring, summer, autumn, and winter. Each season is marked by growth, beauty, decline, and disappearance. And though there are variations and occasional exceptions, the pattern is predictable and immutable.

Modern technology has sought—with an astonishing degree of success—to change these patterns. Innovations in molecular biology, genetics, agriculture, and climatology have spurred hope that even more change is possible. But these changes have created a torrent of social and ethical issues—all consequences of changes sought in the name of progress. This is a complex matter that lends to no easy solution. Antibiotics have saved countless lives since they were introduced seventy years ago. But overuse of those very antibiotics has created the nightmare of drug resistance for which there is no foreseeable answer. Longevity has been extended beyond what anyone could have imagined one hundred years ago. In 1918, the average male in the United States lived forty-seven years. Today he lives seventy-nine years. He no longer dies from malnutrition, poor ventilation, lack of vitamins, and untreatable infections like syphilis, TB, diphtheria, and strep. Today he lives longer but dies slower—and more painfully—from diseases like heart failure, cancer, and Alzheimer's dementia. 'Progress' has become the touchstone word for our generation, and the raison d'être for our lives.

I fear that this mindset has successfully persuaded us that the seasonal boundaries of life can be transcended with impunity. We feel empowered to invoke a scientific Manifest Destiny just as we invoked a political Manifest Destiny in the nineteenth century. We conquered the West—but at an enormous price.

We no longer feel bound by the seasons of life. Little girls are dressed up to look like young women; adolescents have adopted the behavior and burdens of adults; adults have been crushed by the expectations and pressures of a world that is brutally complicated; and old people, at least in our utilitarian society, are viewed as functionally useless, financially draining, and tolerated at best.

There are tasks that must be accomplished and wisdom that must be acquired in each season in order to move on to the next season with confidence, strength, and joy. To learn these tasks and acquire this wisdom takes time, guidance, and a clear understanding of how the building blocks of life fit together. Becoming an adult is not the goal. The goal is to live fully in each season. To play without inhibition, to study and learn without fear of failure, to love unconditionally, to live in the moment, and to seek wisdom in each season—all this teaches us how to become whole and integrated humans.

What are the tasks I must accomplish at this stage of my journey? I have reached the wintertime of life—a time to let go of earlier strivings and conflicts, a time for recollection and summing up. The goals and strategies appropriate for the first half of my life are inadequate for where I am now. Youth is indeed beautiful and to be admired. But youth extended beyond its time is a distortion of reality, and becomes a caricature. I need to ask two questions: 1) who am I? and 2) what do I need to be doing at this time in my life?

To find peace and joy in the midst of personal loss, loneliness, and deteriorating health is a major task for anyone—especially older people. But this is where I am—and this is my task.

Lord, teach us to number our days

that we may get a heart of wisdom.

Psalm 90:12

I have just finished doing something I have put off for a long time: writing my life review—an autobiographical survey of my life from earliest childhood to present. It was, in part, a painful experience because it brought back to memory things I'm not proud of as well as happy things that happened along the way. At the end I asked myself the question: "What have you learned?" "What life lessons are worth remembering?" Though there is nothing profound about these lessons, they are nonetheless mine—wisdom born of the blood, sweat, and tears of eighty-three years. Here is what I have learned:

1. Success is not final and failure is not fatal; it is the courage to continue that counts.

2. Material success is good but insufficient to achieve true happiness and meaning in life.

3. Happiness and joy are not synonymous. You can experience happiness and never know joy, and you can know joy in the midst of great suffering.

4. There is no substitute for hard work, patience, and perseverance.

5. You must measure your worth by your dedication to your path, not by your successes or failures.

6. You can't make it without a few friends. A friend is someone who knows all your faults and loves you, anyway.

7. Love, gratitude, and kindness are the most important virtues in life.

8. To forgive another for a deep hurt is the hardest thing in the world. It is also the most important.

9. Life is about learning to make good judgments in the face of insufficient data. Mistakes are inevitable.

10. The heart of another is a dark forest, always, no matter how close it has been to one's own. It cannot be fully known.

11. One cannot live without faith in someone or something.

I have reached that time of life when it is imperative to "number my days that I might get a heart of wisdom." These eleven lessons—while only a beginning—have given me a place to start.

To experience commonplace deeds as spiritual adventures.

Abraham Heschel

Lord, when did we see you hungry and give you food? When did we see you thirsty and give you something to drink? When did we see you lonely and make you welcome?

And the King will reply:

Whatever you did for these you did for me.

Matthew 25:36

Encountering God in other people is saving my life now.

Barbara Brown Taylor

Despite four years of theological training, serving on the foreign mission field, and pastoring two churches over the last fifty-seven years of my Christian journey, I have never really understood what it means to see God in another person. My Protestant theology has taught me to see God in the lives of saintly men and women throughout history, to see God at work in the church, and to present the claims of Christ to those who don't know Him. But to see God in another human being—any human being—is something different. And yet that is exactly what Jesus meant in the passage in Matthew. And that is what Abraham Heschel and Barbara Brown Taylor are talking about.

These quotes speak to an immutable presence of the Divine in all people. This is reflective of C.G. Jung's conviction that "the religious impulse rests on an instinctive basis and is therefore a specifically human function." And long before Jung, the writer of the Book of Ecclesiastes in the Hebrew Bible declared: "He has put eternity into man's mind." A Divine spark resides in every human being, whether they know it or not.

The followers of Jesus never understood that He was the prisoner, the lonely person, and the sick person waiting to be loved. This is about metaphor as reality. What is a metaphor? A metaphor is a figure of speech in which a term is transferred from the object it ordinarily designates to an object it may designate only by implicit comparison or analogy. The poet Robert Frost once said: "Unless you are educated in metaphor, you are not safe to be let loose in the world." This is especially true for the followers of Christ. Jesus was not physically present in the prisoner. Rather, He was metaphorically present as a Divine revelation worthy of love, respect, and dignity. To see Him in that way requires a new set of eyes—eyes that have learned to see "commonplace deeds as spiritual adventures," as Heschel says. And it is this that made Barbara Brown Taylor realize that acknowledging the presence of God in every person is the core of what it means to walk with Christ.

Indians have a wonderful tradition of bringing the palms of both hands together and raising their hands up to their face whenever they meet and engage another person in conversation. It is a gesture of respect deeply imbedded in their culture.

The historical root of this gesture, however, communicates more than respect. It means: "the God in me greets the God in you." That is, the God who resides in my soul greets the God who resides in your soul. Just as I am a spiritual being, so are you. I find this a gesture of profound spiritual depth and human warmth.

Many people of religious persuasion—regardless of their tradition—suffer from a kind of theological myopia. They can see only the truth and goodness of their own tradition, and dismiss the possibility of truth and goodness in traditions other than their own. This form of tribalism is a curse on all religions because it denies the possibility that God can be found anywhere other than one's own tradition. I repudiate that perspective. God is bigger than my theology because His love and presence encompass all of humanity. The only argument I can offer for the reality of God in my life is to honor the reality of God in your life with love, respect, and dignity.

My crown is in my heart, not on my head;

not deck'd with diamonds and Indian stones, nor to be seen;

my crown is called content;

a crown it is that seldom kings enjoy.

William Shakespeare

The utmost we can hope for in this world is contentment; if
we aim at anything higher, we shall meet with nothing but
grief and disappointment.

Joseph Addison

Be content with your lot; one cannot be first in everything.

Aesop

Who is rich? Only he who is

satisfied with his lot.

Pirkei Avot (Sayings of the Talmudic Fathers)

Over these last few years, it has become increasingly clear that
the task of the wintertime of life is to become wise. True
wisdom has nothing to do with intellectual capacity, and in fact
requires one to leave the realm of "knowledge" in order to
enter the realm of "non-knowledge" (what the Germans call
"*Unwissen*") for the sole purpose of experiencing a new reality
of living characterized by inner peace and serenity. My
education, career goals, and cultural values have not prepared

me for this task. I live in a society that glorifies intellectual achievement, aggression, hard work, monetary success, greed, and power. This is what it takes to make your mark and be recognized as "a winner." To fail in this endeavor is to be a "loser."

To my astonishment, these very benchmarks are of no value in the wintertime of life. In fact, they are a hindrance. C.G. Jung once said:

We cannot live the afternoon of life according to the program of life's morning—for what was great in the morning will be little in the evening, and what in the morning was true will at evening have become a lie.

Like all my successful friends and colleagues, I have no experiential knowledge of that which all the great religions and wise teachers of the world—east and west—are convinced is the heart of wisdom—namely, to be content in the midst of decline, frailty, uncertainty, dying, and death. In fact, for the ancients, the truly rich man is he who has come to the point of being satisfied with his lot in life, whatever it is.

How am I to understand this? Maybe the way to start is to find out what the word 'contented' means. Webster's Dictionary defines 'contented' as "being satisfied with what one has or with one's circumstances." The implications of this statement are enormous for anyone in touch with all the regrets, failures, unfulfilled dreams, sorrows, and losses that accompany a long life. To be human is to know both suffering and joy. The two are inexplicably joined in the human experience. The ancients knew this. And yet they were convinced that beyond the inevitability of pain, despair, and loss, there exists—much like a deep river flowing beneath our consciousness—the capacity for love, peace, and serenity.

One thing is clear: contentment does not mean fantastical reversal of one's circumstances. The pain remains, the loss remains, the disability remains. What changes is one's response to the pain, loss, and disability. Herein lies the difference between 'disease' and 'illness.' The disease is the biological event (e.g., my stroke, my herniated disc). The illness (e.g., my fear, my tendency to catastrophize threatening events, my need for control, or my acceptance of what is) is the mind's response to that biological event. My response will influence how my mind—and to a great extent, my body—responds to the event. Herein lies a secret: while I have no control over my genetic makeup, and little control over the events that crash into my universe and threaten to crush me (the "slings and arrows of outrageous fortune" described by Shakespeare), I do have control over how I choose to respond to those events. That is, in the midst of chaos, I possess the capacity to respond in ways that are either constructive or destructive.

This sounds like a purely intellectual operation. I am persuaded that it is more than that. I can volitionally choose peace and contentment in the midst of distress and experience nothing at all. I know because I have tried that a hundred times, and it hasn't worked. My desire to choose peace is good—but insufficient. Something is missing. What is missing is the phenomenon of "being acted upon" by a power over which I have no control. It is this mysterious power that takes my desire and makes possible a 'letting go' of the existential suffering that lies at the root of the anguish that blocks me from experiencing peace and acceptance. If this is true, then contentment is a grace—a gift that transcends our ability to heal ourselves.

Contentment—the ability to be satisfied with one's lot in life— is a gift from God granted to every person who truly wants to let go, but doesn't know how. The fundamental reason we can't let go is because there resides in our core being an inability to trust the universe that I am known, loved, and cared for in my pain. When we are bereft of being loved, the fear of isolation is overwhelming. We are alone in the universe and must fend for ourselves. The only way to survive is to ward off any threat. And the way to do that is to be in control of our lives every moment. That works quite well until something happens that takes the control out of our hands—like sickness, loss, or failure. When this happens, fear takes over and life becomes unbearable. I desperately want to be released from my suffering, but not at the price of relinquishing complete control of my life. Perhaps this is what Jesus meant when, in the Gospel of John, he warned that unless a grain of wheat falls into the ground and dies, it bears no fruit. I suspect the 'death' he was referring to is my decision to say 'yes' to the death of my self-control.

There is no more profound death than that. Paradoxically, it is that very 'death' that alone frees us to know a peace and contentment not otherwise possible. This is what the ancients of every religion have taught. This is the Kingdom Within, Inner Illumination, Enlightenment, and Nirvana by different names.

How does one move from "wanting to" to "being able to"? The ancients all agree that the key to wisdom is the discipline of silence. The fruit of silence is acceptance, and the fruit of acceptance is contentment. This is an exercise in patience, perseverance, and time. Nothing happens quickly in the inner world of the soul. And that's the rub: in our impatience we want results quickly. It is our ego-driven impatience that blocks the slow process of inner healing. But experience shows that when one learns the discipline of silence, a sense of calm, confidence, and contentment takes hold in the most trying crises and transforms our lives forever. This is not a quid pro quo algorithm whereby I can say: 'If I do this, I will get that.' Instead, it is an exercise in giving up the quid pro quo mindset and launching out into the deep waters of giving ourselves over to the "nothingness" of silence, trusting that one day I will know the inexplicable peace that is the birthright of our humanity.

You can tell whether a man is clever by his answers.

You can tell whether a man is wise by his questions.

Naguib Mahfouz

Here is the question: what is the purpose of my life? No, that's wrong. The right question is: what is the purpose of my life at this moment/time in my life? I have reframed the question because the goals of life differ dependent on the time of life one is in. As a young man, my goal was to get into medical school and fulfill my dream of becoming a physician. In the mid-years, the goal was to become the best physician/educator I could. But now I am in the evening of life, and those earlier goals have been reached and are no longer sufficient. I must have a goal that is appropriate to this time in my life.

Who am I? I am an older man, a widower, a retired physician, a man with a passion for classical music, books, and good conversation, and a desire to serve my community. Above all, I am a Christian with a heartfelt desire to follow Christ in the daily activities of my life.

My goal is no longer to change the world for Christ. I have not a shred of "reformer zeal" left in me—though at one time I did. The days of passing out tracts on street corners, of preaching evangelistic sermons, of trying to convince unbelievers of the sinfulness and folly of their ways—all that is over and has been replaced by a quieter way of life focused on how to live out the principles of love in the spirit of Christ.

Two sayings serve as my guide at this time in my life. The one Jewish, the other Christian. The first was written by Felix Adler and adorns my wall in Hebrew script.

The purpose of man's life is not happiness, but worthiness.

118

The second is a prayer ascribed to St. Francis of Assisi:

Lord, make me an instrument of thy peace.

Where there is hatred, let me sow love,

Where there is injury, pardon;

Where there is doubt, faith;

Where there is despair, hope;

Where there is darkness, light;

Where there is sadness, joy.

O divine Master, grant that I may not so much seek

To be consoled, as to console,

To be understood, as to understand,

To be loved, as to love,

For it is in giving that we receive;

It is in pardoning that we are pardoned;

It is in dying that we are born to eternal life.

Felix Adler's citation reminds me that the ultimate purpose of my life must not be limited to the fulfillment of materialistic goals, but in striving for a higher goal—namely, living a life worthy of God. This echoes St. Paul's admonition to the Colossians: "Lead a life worthy of the Lord."

St. Francis' prayer is a call to live a life of service in personal relationships. This is not about theology. It is a call to serve in the most personal, practical ways imaginable. It is the purest example of St. Paul's compliment to the Christians at Corinth: "All can see that you are an open letter from Christ."

To the question: what is the purpose of this moment in my life's journey, I can answer: to follow Christ by asking Him to make me an instrument of His peace. Nothing more, but nothing less.

Life will give you whatever experience is most helpful for the evolution of your consciousness. How do you know this is the experience you need? Because this is the experience you are having at the moment.

Eckhart Tolle

Step by step, at every step there stands that which is conducive to the next step.

Sanskrit Saying

Night is God's love experienced as pain.

St. John of the Cross

*In the dawn of the day I call to thee
help me pray
direct my thoughts to thee
I cannot manage on my own
it is dark within me, but there is light in thee
I am lonely, but thou wilt not leave me
I am faint of heart, but know thou wilt help me
I am troubled, but know that in thee is peace
I am bitter, but in thee is endurance
I do not understand thy ways
but you understand them for me.*

Dietrich Bonhoeffer

Recently I have been thinking about being content with one's lot in life, and am persuaded that this is not only possible, but a core ingredient of the spiritual life. Yet I struggle with its implications, spelled out in the specifics of a life lived in pain and suffering. The reasoning part of me wonders if this is really possible.

The quotations from Eckhart Tolle, the Sanskrit, and St. John of the Cross are all allusions to an invisible force dedicated to guiding one to a higher level of consciousness. Spiritual masters of all faiths have known this. They have all said what Meister Eckhart said: "Truly, it is in darkness that one finds light."

And yet the darkness can be overwhelming which is why I am so moved by Dietrich Bonhoeffer's prayer. It is a cry of anguish from a true believer caught in a web of circumstances that threatened to undermine the very foundations of his faith. In this he is every person who wants to trust God in darkness.

Bonhoeffer wrote this prayer from prison just days before he was hanged by the Nazis for active resistance against Hitler. His prayer is my prayer because it so poignantly describes the ambivalence of wanting to believe and, at the same time, fearing that the darkness of doubt and failure will overtake him. He says: "I cannot manage, it is dark, I am lonely, I am faint, I am troubled, I am bitter, I do not understand." Who does not know those words? Yet he does not totally yield himself to the darkness that surrounds him. Amidst his pain he claims: "yet." That is an enormous help in my own battles, for it encourages me to continue to believe that although "I do not understand thy ways, you understand them for me." As it was with Bonhoeffer, so it is with me—and all believers—that the way forward spiritually is not by understanding, but by trust and a child-like faith.

When two people relate to each other authentically and humanly, God is the electricity that surges between them.

Martin Buber

All real living is meeting.

Martin Buber

The only thing that really converts people

is the face of the other.

Emmanuel Levinas

I had an amazing experience the other day: I met a lady with whom I had a truly authentic encounter. She lives on the dementia unit in our Nursing Home where I had gone to give devotions. There were about ten residents at the meeting, nine of whom were asleep. But one lady—named Pat—was awake and seemed interested in what I had to say. I talked about the 23rd Psalm and the fear of dying, and began a conversation with her about her life's journey and fear of death. Our conversation must have lasted almost thirty minutes, and by the end, we were fast friends. Despite her cognitive deficits, Pat had remarkable insight into the meaning of her life and her faith. A simple woman, she nonetheless engaged with me in a way that touched me. I left with the unshakable feeling that I had been graced by an authentic encounter with another human being. The fact that she was 95 and had dementia was completely immaterial.

Here is the lesson: **true encounters are always unscripted and unexpected.** When they happen, something powerful takes place that changes each party in ways that cannot be measured, but are real. It made me think of Buber's quote about God and electricity, and his conviction that "all real living is meeting." Life, if it is real, is lived out in relationships, not in isolation. To be sure, solitude and inner reflection are necessary components of true character formation. But the test of that formation lies not in isolation, but in the capacity to give and receive in lasting relationships. We are all converted— i.e., changed—by the face of the other. That is, we are changed at all levels of our being by deep, sustained, and meaningful engagement with the face (the personhood) of the other.

Marriage is the perfect example of this kind of conversion. Marriages that end quickly never have an opportunity to experience the "meeting" that Buber is talking about. Nor the "conversion" that Levinas means. Only those marriages that endure the vicissitudes of life—with their inevitable highs and lows—fulfill the necessary condition for "conversion." The catalyst for all this is time. Nothing of any true substance in life happens quickly. Explosions, insights, inspirations—all those "aha" moments we live for—appear suddenly, as if by spontaneous combustion. But in fact, much work has already been done at the unconscious level, slowly grappling with an unsolved problem in preparation for the moment of clarity. It's only that we are unaware of this inner preparation. It takes years to get to know ourselves—and the other—before we can begin to understand—and correctly appreciate—the depth of our differences and begin to see "the face" of the other. Only then can we "convert" and "be converted."

Life can be perfectly satisfying

without major achievements.

Alice Munro, Nobel Prize Winner in Literature

I came across this quote the same day that I saw an article in the New York Times entitled "Let's Hear It for the Average Child." For someone who has spent his life in a profession that recognizes—and prizes—only the highest level of performance, these two pieces struck me as profoundly true.

The world of success (at least of the "high achievement" variety) can be divided into the following categories:

1. the super-achievers—those who are so enormously gifted that they reach their goal with a modest amount of effort;

2. the achievers—gifted (though not brilliant) who, with sustained effort and perseverance, reach a high level of achievement;

3. the "wannabe" achievers—limited by natural talent but nonetheless capable, hard-working who will never rise to the top, and thus feel intimidated, inadequate, and unfulfilled. They achieve—and in many cases do excellent work—but are frustrated by their limitations. Their greatest curse is that they yearn for a level of accomplishment and recognition that will never be theirs. They "wannabe" someone they are not.

4. the balanced achievers—they know their strengths (which can be considerable) but accept their weaknesses, and have made peace with the fact that they are not cut out for a higher level of achievement. And that's OK with them. These are the people Alice Munro is talking about.

As someone who has spent much of my life feeling like I am in the "wannabe" category, I have come to see that the underlying problem in all this is first, a tragic inability to see the strengths and beauty that one possesses, and second, the high cost of buying into definitions of success established by the world in which we live. Society (i.e., our parents, our educational system, social media, etc.) has an enormous ability to define for us who we are, what our life goals should be, and punish us when we can't reach those goals. The result is that we reach for goals we have not established for ourselves but have been established for us, with the result that we wind up living a life filled with frustration, anger, and poor self-esteem.

For many, a life without a pre-defined major achievement is a life not worth living. It means being satisfied with mediocrity. This is a recipe for despair. Why? Because true major achievements in life are rare. And besides, who decides what a major achievement is? For many, achievement is narrowly defined as a big step up the corporate/professional ladder, wealth, a Nobel Prize, celebrity status. Munro wants to persuade us that this is a warped and delusional definition of achievement, and that if we are willing to redefine our goals— many of which are not attuned to who we are nor correspond to our personal strengths and talent—we can discover a degree of satisfaction and happiness not otherwise possible.

I was educated in a system in which an 'A' is the only acceptable level of academic performance. A 'B' is equivalent to mediocrity and, hence, ultimate failure. That's no problem if you are an 'A' student naturally. But for those of us who are not 'A' students, the fear of failure and the internalization of that fear breeds an inferiority complex that dogs one for a lifetime. Some deal with that fear by becoming a perfectionist—the proverbial over-achiever who can't stop achieving out of a deep-seated fear of failure, and mercilessly flog themselves along the way, or one gives up completely, believing that he simply doesn't have "the right stuff." Both paths are destructive and strangely ignore the fact that a 'B' is not a sign of intellectual mediocrity. 'B' means 'good' in our system. Yet the truth is that not everyone can get an 'A.' If I cannot accept that, despite my best efforts, I cannot get an 'A,' I am doomed to failure. That is simply a horrible way to go through life.

We need to ask ourselves what constitutes "a satisfactory life." And we need to take a good, long look at our God-given strengths and weaknesses. And above all, we need to accept ourselves for who and what we are. Only then can we define for ourselves what we would like to achieve.

Cut off even in the blossom of my sin,

unhouseled, disappointed, unaneled,

no reckoning made, but sent to my account

with all my imperfections on my head:

O, horrible! O, horrible! most horrible!

William Shakespeare

Hamlet, Act I, Sc. 5, l. 74

You may be sure that your sin will catch up with you.

Numbers 32:23

For the last few days, I have been following the trial of Harvey Weinstein, the Hollywood mogul who is being tried for predatory sexual behavior extending over many years. Every time I see his picture on TV, I'm reminded of these two quotations—one from Shakespeare and the other from the Bible.

To see Harvey Weinstein is to see upon a tired, fat, grossly unattractive, sixty-seven-year-old man, and to ask, "Who would want to have sex with him?" I'm reminded of the wonderful lines in George Gershwin's "Porgy and Bess" where Sportin' Life, in singing "It Ain't Necessarily So", says:

But who calls that livin'

when no gal will give in

to no man with nine hundred years?

As pruriently interesting as that question may be, my concern here is the tragic end that is being portrayed—on the global stage of mass media no less—of a man who has come to his day of reckoning for behavior that has grieved and destroyed so many. My deeper concern is the lesson to be learned from this tragedy—a tragedy no less monumental—and universal—than Hamlet.

Dare I say it? Harvey Weinstein is every person. Not perhaps in the specifics of sexual predation, but in the generic sense of harmful behavior which becomes chronic, perpetual, hidden, denied, and eventually so ingrained in our mind that we can no longer help ourselves. One of John F. Kennedy's biographers once asked him why he placed his presidency at risk by womanizing the way he did. His response was: "I simply cannot help myself." Before I criticize JFK (or Martin Luther King, Jr. for the same tendency), I think it is helpful to ask if I am guilty of giving the same answer to the question: what hurtful behaviors do I have that I tend to deny by saying: "that's no big thing," or "that's just me," or "I cannot help it. This is just who I am," or "that's not true."

I know all those excuses, all those denials. I'm Harvey Weinstein—not in specific, but in general. The issue is persistent behavior that hurts others. Things we repeatedly say or do that hurt others. When repeated over time, these things find a home in our mind and become so ingrained in our response pattern that we no longer look upon them (if we ever did) as unusual or hurtful. They have become a part of who we are and how we respond to the world. Harvey Weinstein's predatory mindset has become him. He has acted this way for so long, and with such impunity, that he no longer thinks it's wrong. It is a fixed, unconscious way of getting what he wants. That is pathological. However, what is just as disturbingly pathological is the unrealized tendency for everyone to do the same thing. Maybe it's not sex; but maybe it's money, cheating of all varieties, difficulty with truth-telling, chronic anger, lying. The list goes on. In fact, the list is almost endless. The point is, there is something in the human heart that makes us susceptible to the dark realm of deception and deceit. And when it is not recognized, faced, and dealt with, sooner or later we wind up where Harvey Weinstein is—namely, the man so eloquently described by Shakespeare.

We may pity, though not pardon thee.

William Shakespeare—Comedy of Errors

Forbear to judge, for we are sinners all.
Close up his eyes and draw the curtain close;
and let us all to meditation.

William Shakespeare—Henry VI

The fact alone is always a liar;
it needs to be rounded into full circle,
for fact alone is only part of the truth.

Edwin Markham, poet

But I possess this treasure in a frail vessel of earth.

II Cor. 4:7

Show me how frail I am.

Psalm 39:4

How is one to understand the simultaneous capacity for
profound good and evil?

Colleen Dulle

Every strength of character we admire bears with it a
weakness we must forgive.

Alain de Botton

It is always painful when one of your heroes is shown to have feet of clay. That happened to me this weekend when I heard the news that Jean Vanier—a man of great spiritual stature and reputation throughout the world—has been found to have sexually abused women over the years. Vanier founded the L'Arche homes for social/spiritual rehabilitation for men with cognitive handicaps fifty years ago, and it has grown into an international movement of 154 communities in 38 countries. Vanier died last year and has been considered for sainthood within the Catholic Church—until now. What has come to light is that Vanier seduced a number of women over the years, using the power of his stature to manipulate them into repeated non-consensual and abusive sexual encounters, telling them that this would bring them closer to Jesus and Mary. The women have been deeply wounded and have come forward in light of the #MeToo movement.

I met Jean Vanier in 1985 at Harvard Divinity School. I was deeply moved by his spirituality, his authenticity, and his commitment to the community he had founded. Over the years, I have followed his work closely, heard him lecture, and read many of his writings. I have placed him in my pantheon of "Christian heroes." So I was stunned to hear the news.

His guilt is reputedly beyond question. My task now is to try to put this fact in perspective—a perspective that balances justice with mercy, which is why I have listed the several quotations above. Each one reminds me of something I need to remember in trying to understand how it is possible for a man of Vanier's depth to have hurt so many people.

As I look back on my journey of almost sixty years of service in the church, I am struck by three things: first, until recently, church leadership, whether Catholic or Protestant, has traditionally been in the hands of older men; second, sexual misconduct has always been a problem within the church; and third, church leaders of prominence (whether popes, priests, seminary professors, pastors, evangelists, or charismatic lay leaders) have a well-documented history of sexual predation.

Given this, it is not surprising that the Vanier incident occurred. We are shocked because it is hard to understand how it is possible that godly men can do such ungodly things. One can ask, of course, if these were really godly men. Yet who can deny that Jean Vanier spent his adult life doing truly godly things in his work with the mentally handicapped? If this be so, it raises the discomforting question that Colleen Dulle raises—namely, can it be that buried beneath the surface of genuine goodness and light there exists a dimension of darkness which, if not recognized, can rise to the surface and take the form of deeds of evil to oneself and others?

The Swiss psychiatrist C.G. Jung would have no problem understanding Jean Vanier. Jung would have recognized Vanier as essentially a good man who, in the course of his life and work, cut himself off from his darker side, and in so doing fell prey to destructive impulses, obsessions, and actions. This is both the curse and the destiny of every gifted leader (sacred or secular) whose gifts (remarkable as they may be) are not tempered by the painful lessons of self-insight, wisdom, and humility. Unfortunately, these three qualities are typically not found among leaders. For the religious leader, the task is even more difficult. It is virtually impossible to see one's personal darkness hiding behind the veil of sanctity and righteousness. Everything is legitimized in the name of divinity. Everything is interpreted within the structure and framework of God's working through the life of the "servant." Thus, everything is allowed. This is why the cited verse in Psalm 39: "Lord, show me how frail I am" is so important. Jean Vanier was a man, I believe, who at one time had a vision for good. But somewhere along the way, through a long-standing cultic relationship with his mentor, lost his way—that is, he got carried away by delusions of religious grandiosity that allowed him to violate his soul and the souls of others. He called it Jesus. But it wasn't Jesus. It was—like all pathological delusions—the projection of his distorted ego onto vulnerable women who could not see him for what he was because they were blinded by their own emotional needs.

None of this is an excuse. But it is, I think, an explanation. Jean Vanier, despite the good he did, hurt many people. For this, he will suffer an irreparable loss of respect and reputation. But his work will survive. His is not the first good work to suffer the flaws and failures of its founder. The legacy of L'Arche is greater than the failures of its founder. Strangely, this is also the story of the church. It, too, is "a treasure in a frail vessel" which, because of that very frailty, has suffered greatly over the centuries. But it never dies. I need to remember that.

Jean Vanier was a frail vessel used by God for a specific purpose. But he himself was deeply and mysteriously flawed— as are all of us who seek to serve God. Shakespeare was prescient when he said:

> *Forbear to judge, for we are sinners all.*
>
> *Close up his eyes and draw the curtain close;*
>
> *and let us all to meditation.*

Louange à l'Éternité de Jésus

from

Quartet for the End of Time

Olivier Messiaen—performed by

Yo-Yo Ma and Kathryn Stott

When we have trouble or calamity

is it because He doesn't love us anymore?

And if we are hungry, or penniless, or

in danger, or threatened with death,

has God deserted us? No...

Romans 8:35

It is the end of March 2020, a calamitous and unforgettable time for this country and the world, because the entire planet is being consumed by the Corona virus pandemic. Not since the Spanish Flu pandemic of 1918 has the world seen such a thing. What began in China a few months ago has now engulfed every country on every continent of the globe. And as of yesterday, the epicenter of the infection is in the United States. People have been infected by the millions and died by the thousands from an acute interstitial pneumonia that is staggering in its violence and rapidity. As a country, we are wholly unprepared for this.

As a country, we are shut down, hunkered in our homes with strict instructions to avoid any kind of social contact, urged to wash our hands frequently and avoid touching anything that enters from the outside. These federal mandates, though inconvenient and unnerving, are reasonable. What is maddening is the realization that one can become a vector for the infection without knowing it because it takes several days after inoculation before any symptoms arise, and because there is a paucity of testing available to identify who has the infection and who doesn't. So the only thing one can do is self-isolate, follow the self-care instructions, watch the news for the patterns of spread, and pray that you don't get too close to someone who tests positive for the virus. And all the time wondering if you're going to be next.

The best predictions estimate that this public health crisis will last for several months, and that there will be waves of re-infection necessitating renewed lockdown. Besides the loss of life, the cost to the economy is staggering, to say nothing of massive unemployment rivaling the Great Depression.

In the midst of this scourge, I have had a wonderful experience. I heard Yo-Yo Ma perform Olivier Messiaen's *Louange à l'Éternité de Jésus* and was moved by the transcendent beauty of this small section of his Quartet for the End of Time. It is truly sublime. I have been touched by "the sublime" in music three times in my life. The first time was in 1961 when Pierre Fournier performed the Dvorak Cello Concerto in Zurich; the second time was in Zurich in 1962 when Hans Thomann played the Sarabande from a Bach Suite for Unaccompanied Cello; and the third time was in La Jolla in 1975 when the Guarneri Quartet performed a Beethoven Late Quartet. Each time I was so moved by the music that I could not speak. For hours afterward, I was literally mute. Even now I cannot talk about those experiences with anyone. They are as religious to me as my spiritual experiences. I know now that they, too, were profound religious experiences.

The same thing happened to me the other day when I heard the Messiaen work. I had heard it once before performed by the cellist Fred Sherry. I was impressed but not moved. But Yo-Yo Ma's interpretation was so penetratingly beautiful that it took my breath away in the same way that hearing Bach for the first time in 1962 took my breath away.

The deeper significance of this work lies in the realization that it was composed in a German concentration camp in 1941. In the midst of unthinkable deprivation and dehumanization, Olivier Messiaen, a renowned French composer and a devout Catholic, was able to compose a masterpiece of simplicity, hope, and joy to the eternity of Jesus. When I think about this, I am humbled to my core.

How is it possible to do that? That is only possible if one truly believes Romans 8:35. That is, there is no degree of darkness, pain, or deprivation that can separate us from Christ's love for us. The darkness of night—as horribly dark as it may be—cannot separate us from Him. It is in the darkest part of darkness that Christ is closest to us, to comfort us, to succor us, and to restore us that we might be strengthened in our journey. Messiaen knew that, and in a miraculous way, said that through his music.

As I sit here in the midst of this pandemic, I am both comforted and strengthened in knowing that there is a greater context within which I can—and must—live through this crisis. The over-arching truth of my life is that nothing can separate me from God's love expressed in the eternity of Jesus. Whether the corona virus infects me or not, whether I live or die, He has promised to love me and walk with me through the valley of the shadow of death. To conquer the fear of death is the greatest victory of all.

Some things cannot be fixed; they can only be carried.

Megan Devine

The music is not in my fingers. It's in my mind.

I don't need my right hand for that.

Leon Fleisher

Celebrating the gift of loss.

Kimberly Myers

You desire to know the art of living, my friend?

It is contained in one phrase: make use of suffering.

Henri-Frederic Amiel

Sooner or later one realizes that the most predictable constant in life is change. In common parlance, one says: 'Stuff happens.' Imbedded in that little phrase is the frightening truth that 'stuff' means 'bad stuff.' Bad things can (and often do) happen that are simply beyond our control. They come crashing down on us without warning and we are bereft as to how to deal with it all.

Leon Fleisher, once acclaimed the most talented pianist of his generation, was suddenly befallen by a neurologic disorder of his right hand which forced him to give up his stunningly successful career and find a way to live with his broken body and his broken heart. Seventeen years later, he miraculously recovered the full use of his right hand and was able to reclaim his career and his life. But for seventeen years he wandered from one doctor to the other, desperately seeking help while trying to patch his career together by performing concerts with the left hand, as well as teaching and conducting. What went on inside his head during those seventeen years? To be sure, shock, anger, plea-bargaining with God, despair mixed with hope, a deep desire not to give up. Somehow, in the darkness that surrounds each of us when faced with fear and dread, he came to realize that life was still worth living, and that something positive and meaningful could come out of tragic loss. It is this transformative breakthrough that led him to write: 'There is no doubt that what seemed like the end of the world to me in my little life turned into an opportunity for growth, for expansion, and a widening of horizons.'

Kimberly Myers was at the height of her academic career when she was diagnosed with breast cancer. Only a woman can fully grasp what it means to lose a breast, suffer through the hair loss, fatigue, nausea, vomiting, and cognitive dysfunction that accompany chemotherapy, and at the end live with the fear of recurrence. Yet she, too, was determined to fulfill the Jewish saying: 'May you live until you die.' Like Leon Fleisher, she somehow understood that to live life to the fullest requires great courage, risk-taking, determination, and faith. She also realized that she must decide how to deal with the fear of passive resignation, and that her task was to find a life project that would enable her not to just survive, but thrive amidst the chaos, confusion, and uncertainty of it all. What she did, with the help of a photographer, was to create a photographic exhibit of the stages of her cancer treatment from beginning to end. Each photograph was accompanied by a poem or statement on how she felt at every point along the treatment course. The pictures were both graphic and sublime while her poems rang with truth, beauty, and humor. Her exhibit toured the country and has been a source of inspiration and encouragement to countless women who are themselves facing breast cancer.

So what do Leon Fleisher and Kimberly Myers have in common? This: in the midst of devastating loss, one must find a way to "live." There are things in life that cannot be changed; they must be borne. But they must be borne in the spirit that Seneca described:

Floods will rob us of one thing, fire of another.

These are the conditions of our existence which we cannot change.

What we can do is adopt a noble spirit.

To adopt a noble spirit in the face of great loss is to make use of our suffering.

Respect the old when you are young;

help the weak when you are strong;

confess the fault when you are wrong;

because one day in life you will be old, weak, and wrong.

A Buddhist Teaching

This afternoon I had lunch with a frail, ninety-one-year-old resident of my retirement community. Joanna is an intelligent woman who lives alone and yearns for meaningful social contact. She is a graduate of Penn State University with a degree in ornithology, and can identify any bird in south central Pennsylvania by its color, voice, and flight pattern. In short, she is a biologist with a keen mind but limited physical capacity.

As I sat in the dining room with Joanna, I was struck by how many of the other residents walk slowly and with great difficulty. Fifty years ago, they all walked briskly upright. They were busy raising a family, immersed in a career, happily pursuing life with energy. But all that has changed. Now their bodies are racked with pain, they walk stooped over with a walker or ride in an electric chair, and many wonder why they are still living.

When we were finished eating, I rose to help Joanna with her walker, and followed her as we walked out of the dining room. Walking behind her I was reminded of the above Buddhist saying: 'Help the weak when you are strong.' How can I help Joanna? Have lunch with her; sit and listen to her stories as she repeats herself; inquire about her family and her past; don't get irritated because she eats so slowly; overlook her memory problems; help her getting up and down; walk slowly with her; hug her goodbye; don't forget to call her next month whether you feel like it or not; above all, treat her with patience, respect, and the dignity she deserves.

It is so hard to remember that 'one day you will be old and weak.' Part of the natural defense mechanism of youth is a total unawareness of old age and death. This is as it should be in order that the tasks of the first half of life can be realized. It is only when we reach middle age that we become discomfortingly aware that body and mind are slowing down, and the specter of old age starts to make itself known. Our energy begins to wane, our dreams lose their intensity, the pleasures we sought with such prowess and determination no longer seem as important. In fact, we begin to question life itself and become like Rodin's 'Thinker.' But the thought of becoming old and weak is unthinkable. In fact, we recoil from the idea until, a few years later, it is forced on us.

I am eighty-six, and though slower than I was, I am remarkably healthy and do not consider myself 'old and weak.' Joanna is, but I am not! The idiocy of this reasoning is that it denies the fact that, in reality, I, too, am old and weak. The only difference between us is that she now walks with a walker, moves slower, and is more stooped. But all that will change sooner than I think.

And that's the point: we are all on the same continuum of biological inevitability. We are all sojourners on this planet, all brothers and sisters in the flesh, all one biologic family, and thus all in need of love, affirmation, help, and compassion. I will soon be Joanna. Until then, I must help her with love, patience, and kindness. And hope that one day someone will do the same for me.

When I was young I admired clever people;

now that I am old I admire kind people.

Abraham Joshua Heschel

This is the story of my life. For most of my life I admired, and strove to be like, clever people. Clever in the sense of highly intelligent, creative thinkers or doers, eminently successful in their field of endeavor, hard-working, driven, and uncompromising. I don't know where my desire came from. I know only that the burning desire to 'be like my heroes' was the guiding force of my life.

Who were my heroes? They were not my parents nor members of my immediate family (though my maternal grandfather—whom I did not know—was a renowned physician in Los Angeles, and a cousin on my father's side was an Academy Award-winning screenwriter). My heroes were mainly the famous people in medicine and music: Sir William Osler, Albert Schweitzer, C.G. Jung, Viktor Frankl, Gian Tondury, Pierre Fournier, Pablo Casals, Nadia Boulanger. Each was gifted beyond measure—and I wanted their gift. What I didn't realize was that they were who they were, not only because of their enormous talent, but because they had dedicated their entire life to the perfection of their talent—often to the exclusion of everything else in life.

To have heroes in life—especially if one's heroes are men and women of honor and integrity—is one of the important ways in which we learn to identify noble values. We don't grow from lectures, textbooks, or novels so much as rubbing shoulders with men and women (parents, teachers, colleagues, friends, etc.) who exemplify, in their own lives, the possibility of expanding our horizons. Unfortunately, the opposite can happen when the heroes we choose are men and women of lesser stature. In desiring to be like them, we become like them. When the clever people we admire are themselves evil, their evil poisons our souls. All this to say, we have to be careful whom we admire.

My problem is not the people I admired. My problem is that it took a long time for me to realize that there is more to life than being talented. The truly great people of this world have realized that. They all eventually realized that talent alone does not make one a mature human being. Their talent—regardless of how great—needed to be infused by a vision of what it means to use that talent in order to become a person of compassion, generosity, and kindness.

This is what Abraham Joshua Heschel—a man of unparalleled intellectual capacity—had to discover. It took him years to find that out. In fact, it wasn't until he was old that he saw that. It has taken me a lifetime to discover that same truth. I am old, and only in the last few years have I come to realize that being kind is more important than being clever. I admire clever people. But I admire kind people more.

Finding grace in the awkward humanity of people.

Andy Grundberg, NY Times

I just finished watching the World Series and am once again stunned by the athletic prowess of the players. The strength, the fluidity of their bodies, the ease with which they make the impossible look possible and the difficult look easy is breathtaking. I had the same feeling watching the superb American gymnast Simone Biles in the summer Olympics in Tokyo this year. There is nothing like the grace of youth, nothing like the youthful body, and there is nothing like the youthful mind capable of devouring complex material and doing something creative with it. We were all this way when we were young. We just didn't know how wonderful it was. And we never dreamed it wouldn't last forever!

And it doesn't. Eventually an awkwardness creeps in. The pitcher with the blinding fastball notices a slight change in his speed; the smart decision-maker notices he can't make decisions as quickly as he used to; when she looks into the mirror, she notices the hint of a wrinkle. The sheen wears off, the smooth edge becomes craggy, fast becomes slow—and soon everyone notices. Such is the story of our life—no exceptions.

Our days are few and brief, like grass, like flowers,

blown by the wind and gone forever.

Psalm 103:15

For a youth-worshiping society like ours, this is bad news. It's a double whammy because although we know it happens to everyone, we have no way to handle it when it comes. To lose the beauty and competence of our youth is to lose

145

everything—including our identity. Alas, the wind has blown, and I am gone forever.

The West has no antidote for loss. But the East does. At least the school of Japanese Wabi Sabi does. Wabi Sabi is the Japanese art of impermanence. It is a way of understanding the Zen philosophy of beauty in simplicity. In his book entitled **Wabi Sabi—The Japanese Art of Impermanence**, Andrew Juniper writes:

*The term **wabi sabi** suggests such qualities as impermanence, humility, asymmetry, and imperfection. These underlying principles are diametrically opposed to those of the Western counterparts, whose values are rooted in a Hellenic worldview that values permanence, grandeur, symmetry, and perfection.*

What wabi sabi sees in art is what it sees in humanity—namely, there is beauty in brokenness. It doesn't pretend that there is no awkwardness or imperfection. It is simply able to transcend that two-dimensional view to see something else—namely, beyond brokenness lies beauty.

This view of seeing beauty in imperfection and impermanence has revolutionized my thinking about myself and my aging friends and neighbors. To grow old is not easy. It can be (and much of the time is) excruciatingly difficult. The temptation is to become bitter and pine for the 'good old days' of our youth. This is understandable. But it offers no help. Things are what they are. Better to re-frame our present world and look for another way to live with our losses, our pain, and our brokenness.

The great French Impressionist Auguste Renoir was afflicted with severe rheumatoid arthritis during the last years of his life. He was in constant pain, bound to a wheelchair, and could only paint painstakingly slow by having a long stick attached to his brush to reach the canvas. One day Matisse asked Renoir why he kept on painting when it caused him such pain. He said to Matisse:

The pain passes but the beauty remains.

To see beauty beyond one's own brokenness, to see beauty beyond the outer brokenness of the other, is to see the face of God.

The price of a longer life has been a sicker life.

Daniel Callahan

The truth of these words comes home to me every time I visit my hospice patients. Most of these people are dying from the debility of dementia, heart failure, or malignancy. Some are in pain, while others are detached from reality. Some lie quietly in bed, others moan and scream. All of them are suffering an indecent and undignified end to their life. What can I do? I try to relieve their pain and agitation, treat their infections, and comfort their families. But for the most part, I watch them move inexorably down the road to their demise.

I feel anger—maybe even rage—about this. It's not that I want to cure them. I accept the biological inevitability of death—theirs and mine—in the cosmic scheme of things. It's not that they die, but the way they die that is difficult to bear.

It was not always so. One hundred years ago, the main causes of death were infections, accidents, or injury. Death was violent but mercifully fast. Today it is different. Thanks to modern science, people live longer, and as long as their health is good, better lives. But once they begin to falter, they will die slowly and painfully from a chronic disease like heart failure, stroke, cancer, or dementia.

My pulmonary patients gasp for air, my cardiac patients don't have the energy to walk to the bathroom, my stroke patients have to be toileted, my dementia patients sit staring into space and have to be fed, my renal patients spend three days a week hooked up to a dialysis machine. The nursing staff is wonderful, moving from room to room with words of encouragement, doing the mundane (and often disgusting) tasks of patient care—tasks no one in their right mind would do unless they loved that person or couldn't get another job.

But I struggle with the unanswerable question of why this must be. Why does any human being have to end up like this? I don't know the answer. And neither does anyone else. In the meantime, I need to get on with doing the only thing I know to do. But the question gnaws at me.

We can be with another in his or her suffering,

and we can try to share it, but we cannot relieve it.

Daniel Callahan

This morning I saw one of my favorite hospice patients. Jim is an eighty-year-old gentleman dying of heart failure. He is dying the way all heart failure patients die: slow and agonizing.

As I have followed the course of his decline, I have been struck by how difficult some deaths are. Some patients—particularly those with a malignancy—go quickly. They are well for a while, and then suddenly something happens—usually an infection—that brings about a rapid decline and death. Others, like Jim, go slowly. They rally for a while, then relapse, then improve, and finally remain in a slow, painful, steady decline. And always there is the shortness of breath, chest pain, and fatigue. So it has been with Jim. I've tried everything. But there is nothing left to work with. The only thing now is morphine—enough to keep him sedated while he marches inevitably toward his death.

In the last several weeks, Jim has begun to suffer—not just from fatigue, but from despair. He knows he is dying, and that there is not much more that can be done. He is a gracious man and is grateful for everything we have done. But now all he can do is lie there and wait. To lie in bed day after day, with no hope for change, is corrosive to the soul. He has significant spiritual resources and is a man of faith. But chronic illness exhausts the mind and body so thoroughly that one is stripped of all his defenses and loses hope. All he—and his family and caregivers—can do is pray for an end to this torture.

I left Jim this morning with deep sadness—a sadness born of my desire to relieve his suffering. I have seen so many patients like Jim over the years, and have always felt helpless. As I pondered this, I thought of Dan Callahan's sober reminder that we cannot relieve another person's suffering. Suffering is more than a physical symptom—though unrelieved pain will create suffering. It is the soul's unique and personalized response to the "slings and arrows of outrageous fortune," and may have little to do with its objective cause. Because suffering is a response of who we are as a whole person, it is not wholly open to our ministrations. In the end, I can relieve his pain, but not his suffering. I can lighten his load a bit. But I cannot relieve his deepest burden. My desire to do so is admirable. But wisdom warns me of my boundaries.

Why do some people suffer, and others (often with the same disease process) do not? How is it that some can tolerate great pain, and others cannot? How is it that some collapse under the slightest burden, and others are able to bear enormous burdens?

The obvious explanation would be the differences in temperament and degree of psychological resilience. While that is a plausible explanation, I suspect there is more to it than that. The capacity to suffer is shaped and developed by our view of the universe, and the values that define who we are and what we hold dear. If I am all alone in the universe and have a philosophy that rests on maximizing pleasure and minimizing pain, then suffering possesses no inherent value and is to be avoided at all costs. If, on the other hand, suffering is an integral part of my Weltanschauung, and inherently valuable to the growth and development of who I am as a whole person, then my response is completely different. It is no longer seen as something to be avoided, but to be embraced as the path I must follow on my journey to wholeness. It is to be embraced, not in the sense of actively seeking it. To seek suffering is masochistic and thus unhealthy. Rather, it is to be embraced in the sense of an inner acceptance. This willingness to accept that which is painful is inevitably accompanied by difficulty and a profound (and sometimes prolonged) sadness. But the truth is, because it is a part of life, it is a part of my life. If I accept it and don't run away from it, my suffering mysteriously becomes the vehicle by which I am transformed into a person of greater depth, understanding, and strength. It is the alchemy of the soul.

I wanted to take Jim's suffering from him. That would have been a mistake. Only he can enter the valley of the shadow of death where the body, mind, and soul are clarified. No one can accompany another at that point. The soul is alone with God and can't be deterred by the well-meaning, but misguided, desires of those who cannot accompany him on his final journey. In the end, we all die alone.

Guru Nanak called us to see no stranger,

Buddha to practice unending compassion,

Abraham to open our tent to all,

Jesus to love our neighbors,

Muhammad to take in the orphan.

Valarie Kaur

I have just recently finished Valarie Kaur's book **See No Stranger,** and through it have been introduced to the Sikh religious faith. I have known nothing of Sikhism other than that Sikh men wear turbans. Added to my ignorance, I have assumed that Sikhism is a branch of Hinduism. Wrong! Though both faiths stem from India, they are not the same.

The book is the story of Valarie Kaur's journey to find her place in society as an American Sikh, and to find herself as a Sikh woman. It is a remarkable story told by a remarkable woman. More important were her comments about Guru Nanak, the founder of Sikhism. His teaching that we are 'to see no stranger' is so powerful and all-encompassing that it took my breath away. As she says: 'The call to love beyond our own flesh and blood is ancient.' Ancient Hindus say: '*Tat Tvam Asi,*' 'I Am That'; African philosophy says: '*Ubuntu,*' 'I am because of you'; the Mayan precept says: '*In La'Kech,*' 'You are my other me.'

The universality of this precept shakes me to the core because 'love,' 'equality,' and 'compassion' did not originate with any one religion, nor are they the possession of any one religion, one nation, or one tribe. They are the core of who we are as human beings.

The great tragedy is that while we recognize the importance of these qualities in building a society of civility and uprightness, we seem unable to 'operationalize' them in any consistent, meaningful way. That is, we cry out for love while at the same time we go to war. It is as St. Paul says in Romans 7:21:

It seems to be a fact of life that when I want to do what is right, I inevitably do what is wrong. Oh, what a predicament I'm in!

The Christian solution to this unending problem is to come to grips with sin and turn to Christ as the only way to become free from the power—though not the presence—of sin. This is not what I want to develop in this writing. Rather, I want to reflect on the universal call to love and to 'see no stranger.' This call is not unique to the Abrahamic faiths (Judaism, Christianity, Islam). It is an ancient call, imbedded in all the major faiths of the world.

Why am I so struck by this? I think it is because I do such a poor job seeing my 'neighbor'—whom I do not know and who may offend me in one way or another—as anything other than a stranger. That is, I am so often unable to accept him into my heart as a fellow sojourner worthy of dignity, respect, patience, compassion, and the kind of 'agape' love that Jesus talked about. And here is the kicker: 'agape' love is exactly what Guru Nanak, and all the other ancients, talked about. The 18th-century English writer Samuel Johnson once said:

Kindness is in our power even when fondness is not.

This is the heart of it: emotional closeness (what Johnson calls 'fondness') is neither possible nor required in meeting the stranger. But 'kindness' (that is respect, tact, dignity, compassion) is. The secret is: once I show kindness to the stranger, he becomes a person and no longer a stranger.

I long to be able to 'see no stranger' more often than I do in my daily life. Dag Hammarskjold, the great statesman, poet, and mystic, once wrote: 'If only I may grow firmer, simpler, quieter, warmer.' I would add to his prayer, for myself: 'If only I may see no stranger.'

We need a charity, but not of the usual kind;

we need what we might term a 'charity of interpretation';

that is, we require an uncommonly generous

assessment of our idiocy, weakness, eccentricity, or deceit.

Alain de Botton

Just as a mother has compassion for her child,

so do you have compassion for those who hold you in awe.

For you know our inclinations

and remember that we are dust.

Psalm 103:13-14

I am struck by the fact that no matter how hard I try to please God in my daily life, I fall prey to the old ways of my human failings and limitations. In other words, I am a recidivist. There is nothing new or unique in this statement. The Apostle Paul himself struggled with this painful reality when he wrote in Romans 7:21: 'I desire to do what is right, but wrong is all I can manage.' He goes on to write in verse 25: 'Thank God there is deliverance through Jesus Christ our Lord!' I have not found that to be the case. The tendencies I had sixty years ago, when I became a Christian, still dog me. The only difference is that now I feel great guilt and shame—but no deliverance despite heartfelt belief.

All this has led me to consider the question of deep-seated tendencies in the human personality that become so 'fixed' in our thinking and behavior that they resist any attempt at removal. It is for this reason that I chose Pamela Greenberg's translation of Psalm 103—in particular, her use of the word 'inclination' in verse 14. It seems to me that each of us has 'inclinations'—that is, strange, sometimes aberrant ways of thinking and acting—that may have genetic roots, but are, to a great extent, the product of the values and emotional health of the most important people in our lives in our formative years—namely our parents and the social/cultural milieu in which we are raised. We are not a tabula rasa, but rather an accretion of conscious and unconscious influences which harden over the years to become personality traits. It is the combination of these traits that makes us who we are.

The question now is: Can these traits be changed? Can we become someone we are not? The answer is 'yes and no.' An authentic religious commitment (regardless of what faith tradition) can change a person in dramatic, life-altering ways. History has borne this out repeatedly. So the answer to the question is 'yes' if we mean life-altering, but 'no' if we mean personality-altering. Some behaviors change immediately, some change slowly, and some behaviors and ways of thinking will never change for reasons we do not understand. It is this third category that frightens us, frustrates us (and others around us), humbles us, and makes us doubt God's power and sufficiency.

And yet, despite the painful residual, the changes are monumental. Despite my weaknesses and recidivism, God has unmistakably changed my life. Where I was once utterly self-centered, God has created an other-centered person. In my attempt to follow Christ, I have become patient, kind, and compassionate—traits not characteristic of the driven person I used to be. Yet there remains an unalterable core of thinking and behavior that eludes my attempts to change. These are 'my inclinations, my eccentricities, my weaknesses, my idiocy.' I don't like it, I'm embarrassed and ashamed of it. But it is what it is. And unless God's grace changes it, it will remain.

This is why I feel drawn to Alain de Botton's idea of 'charity of interpretation.' It is based on the fact that, in the final analysis, we are who we are. In light of that, we are asked to accept one another in spite of our strangeness and shortcomings. What de Botton doesn't say (nor may believe) is that God accepts us in our strangeness and shortcomings. Why? Because He knows that we are dust. That is, we are imperfect by our very nature and live awkward, incomplete lives. What is astounding is that God knows my oddities and imperfections and is not ashamed of them. He loves me in spite of myself. It is this knowing-it-all and loving me in spite-of-it-all that religion calls 'agape'; de Botton calls it 'charity of interpretation.' Either way, it is a call to accept ourselves in our imperfections, and to accept others with 'a generous assessment' of their imperfections.

I'm calling to let you know that when we visit tomorrow

you will not recognize Greg.

He has dementia just like both his parents did.

Leesa

We are dying, we are dying, so all we can do is now to be

willing to die, and to build the ship of death to carry the soul

on the longest journey.

D.H. Lawrence

Seventy years are given to us! And some may live to eighty.

But even the best of these years are often emptiness and

pain; soon they disappear, and we are gone. Teach us to

number our days, and recognize how few they are; help us to

spend them as we should.

Psalm 90:10-12

This morning Leesa called to tell me that Greg has been diagnosed with probable Parkinson's Dementia, and that he has lost much of his cognitive capacity. They are both scheduled to join me for lunch tomorrow to talk about retirement community possibilities. It has been some time since Greg and I last had lunch (an almost monthly ritual), and

159

knowing that, she did not want me to be shocked at the changes I will see. I was shaken to the core at this news. Greg is a dear friend and colleague and was, at one time, my personal physician. He is a man of immense talent and a decent person with a genuine faith and faithfulness to his Church. The news of his diagnosis is a painful reminder of the inevitability of life's course. Death comes to us all and is almost always preceded by a slow (or sometimes fast) process of dying. For Greg, given his genetic predisposition, the course is set. The only unknowns in the equation will be the length of time he will have to suffer, and the specifics of his individual suffering. But the path is marked out.

As a hospice physician, I have taken care of hundreds of dying men and women. I know what to expect, and have learned to steel myself from the pain that they and their families go through. It is one of the 'acquired skills' of taking care of sick people, to be close enough to the patient's pain to feel their distress, but not so close that it overwhelms you. Unless one learns that, one will be crushed by the immensity of suffering that confronts one every day. I have learned that skill, as has every experienced physician. But once in a while—a loved one, a close friend, a child, a colleague—the pain and injustice of it comes crashing in, and overwhelms even the most experienced of us. This is what happened to me this morning. Leesa's call, telling me that Greg has been struck down by this dreadful disease, caught me off guard, frightened me as much as grieved me, and reopened a wound in my own heart about the fear of death and dying we all share.

D.H. Lawrence wrote about building 'the ship of death' for his soul a few weeks before he died of tuberculosis. I take his phrase 'ship of death' to mean a place in his heart (an 'attitude' perhaps) where he could retreat and find meaning and strength for what he foresaw as a long journey for his soul. This is the poetic language of a man who knows he is going to die, and can no longer put off the inner work of preparation for a journey he knows nothing about, but knows that it is approaching.

This is exactly what I think the psalmist is saying when he urges us to number our days. Why number our days? In order that we might live as we should in the few that are left. Whether we like it or not, our days are few. It doesn't seem like that when you're young. But in mid-life one starts to get 'intimations of immortality'—suspicions that hard work, success, family, community standing, and wealth are good, but somehow not fulfilling; there must be something more to life. That rather unwelcome suspicion is at first put off to the side, and one settles in to work harder 'for the future of the kids.' But as one enters the sixties, health issues remind us that 'time is of the essence.' The words of Kurt Weill's 'September Song' take on an uncomfortable poignancy:

Well, it's a long, long time

From May to December

But the days grow short,

When you reach September.

And the autumn weather

Turns the leaves to gray

And I haven't got time

For the waiting game.

And the days dwindle down to a precious few...

September, November...

When one loses a loved one or close friend, something inside us grieves, for when he/she dies, a part of me dies. This is clearly what John Donne meant when he wrote:

Every man's death diminishes me,

Because I am involved in mankind.

Greg is dying. A part of me is grieving and dying. The only way I know to grieve is to journey as closely as I can with my friend, and to ask God to help me build my own little ship of death by numbering my days "that I might spend them as I should."

Who are you?

I am an alcoholic

Joe Clay in "Days of Wine and Roses"

Who am I? 2-4-6-0-1.

Jean Valjean in "Les Miserables"

Victor Hugo

The willingness to accept responsibility for one's own life is the source from which self-respect springs.

Joan Didion

Each one of us is more than the worst thing we've ever done. No one is just the crime he or she commits.

Bryan Stevenson

Last week I was watching the movie "Days of Wine and Roses" (1962) about an inveterate alcoholic who found release and a new life through AA. The movie, excellently acted by Jack Lemmon and Lee Remick, was the story of an alcoholic couple who lose everything. But there was one scene that spoke to me so powerfully that I have thought about it ever since. It was Joe Clay's (the character played by Jack Lemmon) first AA meeting. It is protocol in all AA meetings that when a new member joins, he/she introduces himself and then says: "I am an alcoholic." Lemmon brilliantly portrayed the ambivalence and shame Joe struggled with in getting those four words out. To say publicly, "I am an alcoholic" created such emotional nakedness that Joe wanted to avoid it, but knew he couldn't. It was a moment of truth—the kind of painful truth we all try desperately to avoid when admitting to ourselves—and the world—that we are guilty of whatever we have done. And yet, speaking that truth was just what was required for Joe to begin his healing.

As I have pondered that, I have had to ask myself: Why did that scene so arrest me? Not only arrest me, but sink so deep in my heart? There was something about the expression on Joe Clay's face, and the utter honesty of his words "I am an alcoholic" that was more than intellectual acknowledgment or even "being touched" by the poignancy of the moment. There was something highly personal about that moment that caught me off guard.

I had the same response to the moment in "Les Mis" when Jean Valjean, a parolee who had done his time in prison for stealing bread. He disappeared from parole, changed his name, and over the years became a respectable member of a community—even rising to be the mayor—when he was suddenly confronted by his past. In a moment of anguish, he cried out: "Who am I? 2-4-6-0-1," which was his prison number. The past he ran away from eventually came back to haunt him.

Joan Didion's stern reminder that until we take full responsibility for who we are, will we never have a sense of self-respect. It is this "taking responsibility" that forms the common denominator between Joe Clay and Jean Valjean.

And yet, as Bryan Stevenson reminds us, we are more than the worst thing(s) we have done. We are, in fact, a mysterious mixture of sacred and secular, light and dark, good and bad, right and wrong. Stevenson knows whereof he speaks. As Founder and Executive Director of the Equal Justice Initiative in Montgomery, Alabama, he has defended hundreds of men and women in the Alabama prison system. Through that, he gained intimate knowledge of these people—the good, the bad, and the ugly—and has concluded that there is more to a human being than the worst acts one has ever done.

How am I to understand all this? Can I really know myself, in the Socratic sense, without being so crushed that life is no longer worth living? Do I have the moral courage to see the dark side of my personality without denying it? And if I see it and accept it, can I put it into a perspective that allows me to recognize (and embrace) that what I have seen—though true—is not the totality of me? The prophet Jeremiah would conclude otherwise—that at root there is only darkness: "The heart is deceitful above all things, and desperately corrupt; who can understand it?" (17:9). And St. Paul would echo this in his letter to the Romans.

In Christian theology, darkness is our fate given the Fall. It is only through the gift of Christ, who came to expiate our sins, that forgiveness and redemption are possible. In the Christian view, Joe Clay is without hope beyond confessing that he is an alcoholic. While confession is the first and necessary step, he must accept God's invitation of freedom by accepting Christ's invitation to follow Him in trust and obedience. Bryan Stevenson might agree with that position by declaring that he sees what God sees, namely, a scarred, fractured human being in whom resides something precious and worth redeeming. Perhaps Stevenson sees the soul inside the broken heart and knows that the soul is the best part of that person. Maybe he means that beyond our ugly acts, there is something precious that makes us truly human, and that we must never lose sight of that ineffable core. He would agree that Joe Clay and Jean

Valjean are guilty of their shortcomings. He would also agree, I'm sure, that healing begins with contrition and confession. But beyond confession is not damnation, but the potential for redemption. Why? Because the core of each of those people is not their acts, but their soul; and because the soul is pure, it must be allowed to live and flourish.

How to move from darkness to light, from damnation to redemption, is the sole purpose of religion. It has always been so because this is who man is: a creature born into a world he does not understand, shackled to a body and mind over which he has no control, and fearful of a future he dimly perceives. He thinks he is self-sufficient, but eventually realizes he is not, and finally asks: "Isn't there more to life than this?" Or, as St. Paul cried out: "The good I want to do, I don't do; and the evil I don't want to do, I do. Is there no way out?" It seems to me that, over the history of mankind, every culture has attempted to answer that question. The vocabulary has been different, and the expressions and understanding have been different. But the goal has always been the same—namely, how to reach the Divine in bringing meaning and consolation to the human experience.

We are not all so different from one another as we think. Once one gets beyond the barriers of race, culture, language, age, and gender, the human heart—in all its dreams, aspirations, and fears—is remarkably similar, if not identical. Ancient literature from all cultures bears this out. The Mayan precept "*In La'Kech*" ("You are my other me") is profoundly true. This is important for me to remember. Beyond my western education, my career, and my success lies the ineffable core of who I am. That core inside me is the identical core inside every other human on this planet. We are all seeking truth, meaning, forgiveness, and hope.

The answer to the question, at the top of this reflection, "Who Are You?" is that I am Everyman—a man who knows that he is Joe Clay and deeply regrets the implications of that truth. But also a man who seeks to live his life on a higher plane of self-awareness, forgiveness, and hope—a plane where the sacred infuses the mundane of my daily life.

Strokes affect different portions of the brain and can lead to dysfunctions of many types and severities.

Louis Kaplan, M.D.

You must not judge by the appearance of things but by the reality.

John 7:24

I have a friend who had a stroke, recovered, and returned to work. One day, while walking down the hallway, he encountered a colleague who spoke to him. My friend did not acknowledge him and kept on walking. His colleague felt snubbed and broke off their friendship. What the colleague didn't know is that my friend never "saw" him. Why didn't my friend see him? The reason is that my friend's stroke had altered his neural pathways so that he was no longer able to "recognize" his colleague as someone he knew. What he saw was a stranger walking down the hall. That is, he visually **saw** a person, but did not **recognize** him as someone he knew. This is what a stroke can do to one's perception of the world in which they work and live. Unless one understands this, one can draw erroneous conclusions about why certain people do and say what they do.

I think I am keenly aware of this because of my own stroke seven years ago. By comparison, it was a mild stroke affecting my speech pattern, voice, leg strength, balance, tremor, and fatigue. Although I have largely recovered, I am aware that certain changes are permanent, and that I am now dependent on the kindness of others to help me do things I can no longer do for myself. I stay close to friends who know me and are not shocked when I spill my food because of the tremor, who quietly offer their arm when going downstairs and off curbs, who help me on with my overcoat, knowing I can't do it by myself.

My disabilities have served to enlighten me in two ways: First, they have given me a profound understanding and appreciation for what it means to be handicapped. Through this, has come a tenderness and a sense of *Mitgefühl* (feeling with) for every older person I meet. I know what they are going through, their humiliation, helplessness, anger, and fear of being denigrated and misjudged by what they can no longer do.

Second, they have taught me the danger of superficial judgment. That is, judging by appearances only. Almost always, there are other possible explanations for the strange and oft offensive things we hear or see (or do) in our relationship with family, friends, and coworkers. This is what happened to my friend in the hallway. It was not incumbent on his coworker to understand all the neural abnormalities of a stroke. But it was incumbent on him to say to himself: "That's strange, he ignored me. I wonder what is going on." Once we say that, we have moved from judgment to curiosity.

I wonder why it is so hard for us to look beyond the surface in our judgments. I suspect it has much to do with judgments developed (and concretized) over the years—judgments influenced by the biases of our parents, our culture, our education, and our life experiences. The majority of those biases never get challenged or updated. They sadly become who we are. Maya Angelou certainly had this in mind when she said:

Most people don't grow up; most people just age.

Losses and Gains in Aging

And did you get what you wanted from this life, even so?

I did.

And what did you want?

To call myself beloved, to feel myself beloved on earth.

Raymond Carver, "Late Fragments"

Aging is the wintertime of life—the leaves have fallen, the trees are bare, the temperature is cold, snow blankets the ground, and everything has become quiet. Spring with its promise of beauty and blossom, summer with its heat and intensity, autumn with its majestic fullness and unique autumnal beauty have all passed. Now is the time for rest and silence.

The universality and rhythm of this sequence is as old as time itself. All the great religions of the world speak eloquently of this. For example, the psalmist writes in Psalm 103:

Man's days are like grass;

he blossoms like the flowers of the field:

wind passes over them, and they cease to be,

and their place knows them no more.

The first half of life is marked by the intensity of preparation, accomplishment, contribution, and procreation. The tools required are hard work, focus, and determination in reaching hard-won personal and professional goals. The second half of life is different. The tools needed in the first half of life are no longer useful. In fact, the very tools of competitive striving and hard work, so necessary in the first half of life, turn out to be counterproductive in the second half of life. Here, a new orientation is needed—one based on "letting go" and learning to become inwardly quiet. The problem is, in our western society there is no preparation for this. Hence, our losses are seen as catastrophic and our life becomes useless when we can no longer achieve in the ways we are used to. The inevitable illnesses of old age remind us of our seeming decrepitude and reinforce the conviction that there is nothing left to live for. Life ended when we retired.

The losses of aging are obvious. The question in my mind is, are there any gains in aging? And even further, if there are gains, what are they, and do they outweigh the losses? The Jewish Publication Society of America translates Psalm 103:5 to read:

> *He satisfies your old age with good things;*
>
> *so that your youth is renewed like the eagle.*

And the Talmudic saying:

> *For the unlearned old age is winter;*
>
> *for the learned, the season of harvest.*

How am I to understand this? How can it be that, in the midst of the profound losses of growing old, He satisfies my old age with "good things"? What good things? Asking this question is the equivalent of the question asked by Raymond Carver in his poem "Late Fragments":

> *Did you get what you wanted from this life, even so?*

The two words "even so" are telling. These two words, as a phrase, are not used very often today. They mean: "despite everything" or "nevertheless." So today we would translate the line as:

Despite everything you've been through,

did you get what you wanted from this life?

His answer was: "Yes."

In the process of decision making, where we all live on a day-to-day basis, one uses the "benefit/burden ratio" concept in deciding how and what we do. If the benefit of a situation outweighs the burdens, we make a certain decision; if the burden becomes so heavy that it outweighs the benefit, we make another decision. Common examples are decisions to stay or leave a marriage, to change jobs, to choose a college, to make an investment, to discipline a child. The list is endless because the need to make decisions in life is endless. At the root of it all is the evaluation of "gains vs. losses." In fact, most of life is about how to make these kinds of trade-offs in order to survive.

I am now eighty-eight years old and have been pondering the question that Raymond Carver raises. In answer to his "even so," can I answer the question in the affirmative? In order to do that, I need to list the specific losses I have endured as a function of getting old, and then ask myself what, if any, "gains" there are on the other side that would allow me to say "yes."

Losses

The physical losses of aging are heartbreaking and overwhelming. No organ of the body is spared the ravages of the aging process. Whether it is the heart (CHF), the kidneys (CKD), the brain (stroke, Alzheimer's), the musculoskeletal system (arthritis, especially of the spine, falls and fractures), or organ failure due to malignant invasion, the end result is the same: unrelenting pain, difficulty breathing, immobility, cognitive decline, depression and despair. No one is spared.

My own losses include:

1. chronic post-stroke fatigue which has robbed me of most of my energy

2. post-stroke balance problems which make walking both difficult & precarious

3. post-stroke speech pattern alterations—I slur my speech at times

4. post-stroke vocal cord paralysis, which has robbed me of a normal speaking voice & causes me to cough and expectorate constantly

5. post-stroke memory loss—has been creeping up for years, but the stroke has made it much worse

6. post-stroke weakness in both legs, which has brought all travel to an end

7. post-stroke excessive salivation (drooling)

8. urinary urgency

9. atrial fibrillation

10. coronary artery disease

11. tremors (intention on the right side & post-stroke Parkinson on the left side) which robbed me of my cello and all other fine motor activity

12. a certain post-stroke "blunting" of my cognitive ability. Most people do not notice this, but I do. I can function, but I am no longer intellectually facile

13. a kind of social disengagement (more like "disinterest") which I can hide fairly well for short periods of time. Social gatherings & meetings no longer interest me, nor do I tolerate them very well. On the other hand, I greatly enjoy conversations with individuals. I'm reminded of William James:

I am done with great things and big plans, great institutions

and big success. I am for those tiny, invisible,

loving forces that work from individual to individual...

When I review this list, my losses are not what many of my friends and neighbors have to live with. I'm not in constant pain, I can still get around without a cane or walker, I can still drive, I remain intellectually intact, and I enjoy meaningful conversations with friends. Notwithstanding, my losses have come with a price and portend other losses to come. The words that come to mind when I think about this are: sad, awkward, annoying, embarrassing, painful, fear of another stroke, fear of losing my mind and my independence. My apartment is my castle and my refuge. I am surrounded by the things I love (music, art, books). When I look at my paintings and memorabilia on the wall of my study, I am moved by the mystery and richness of my journey. The thought of leaving this makes me very sad.

Gains

Beautiful are the youth

whose rich emotions flash and burn,

whose lithe bodies filled with energy and grace

sway in their happy dance of life;

and beautiful likewise are the mature

who have learned compassion and patience,

charity and wisdom.

But most beautiful and most rare is a gracious old age

which has drawn from the skill to take its varied strands:

the harsh advance of age, the pang of grief,

the passing of dear friends, the loss of strength,

and with fresh insight, weave them into a rich and gracious

pattern all its own.

This is the greatest skill of all,

to take the bitter with the sweet and make it beautiful,

to take the whole of life in all its moods,

its strengths and weaknesses,

and make one great and celestial harmony.

Robert Terry Weston

The ancients of every religion have echoed Robert Terry Weston's sentiments—namely, there is a beauty and richness available in the last stage of life which is not dependent on our circumstances for their expression. In fact, it might be argued that the existence of such a dimension is, in fact, a biologic "given," but is dependent for its expression on the spirituality of the culture in which one finds himself.

Human behavior teaches two things: (1) life consists of a mysterious admixture of bitterness and sweetness; and (2) one of the tasks of life is to learn how to blend the two together. In fact, the work of blending may be THE task of the last stage of life. This brings me back to Carver's question: "Even so, did you get what you wanted from this life?" The answer lies in what it is I really want from life. In my earlier years, what I wanted was to be a competent, caring physician. That goal has been met and is not what I want now. What I want now is "to take the bitter with the sweet and make it beautiful... and make one great and celestial harmony." I have begun that process and feel that I am on a journey that is teaching me that— despite my tendency to fixate on the dark side of life and faith, the gains really do outweigh the losses. To be sure, gains do not abolish the losses. "Even so" understands this. But it transcends the lamentation of loss to allow a wider, more inclusive perspective of reality. The great French Impressionist painter Monet once said:

Color is my obsession—my joy and my torment.

Life is both light and dark, joy and torment. To answer Carver's question in the affirmative requires that I move beyond my painful experiences and limited interpretations to a higher level of understanding that can accommodate both joy and sorrow in forging a new definition of what it means to be fully human.

Maya Angelou once said: "Most people don't grow up, they just grow old." I want to grow up. I want to answer Carver's question in the affirmative by being kinder, more understanding, more forgiving, more patient, more loving, and, above all, more grateful. In doing this, I will grow and be able to "call myself beloved and feel myself beloved on earth."

Too long a sacrifice can make a stone of the heart.

W. B. Yeats

We've been at this for twenty years. Twenty years of seeing a loved one reduced to immobility, dependency, despondency and dementia. In short, an impoverishment of body, mind, and soul.

What I've noticed—to my dismay—is a corresponding impoverishment within my own soul. Against my will there has developed an affliction that might be called "compassion fatigue." This is what Yeats may mean, it is not that love has disappeared, but that the drain of sacrifice has changed it into something different. It is no longer the love I knew, but devotion mixed with pity, sadness and obligation. Maybe this is a deeper form of love, one devoid of romance, and defined by the twin duties of steadfastness and commitment. I don't know. I know only that the essential ingredient of companionship has been taken from us. And with that has come a kind of death to the relationship we once knew. I love her—as the psalmist says—"as a father loves and pities his child, for he knows our frame, and remembers we are dust." It is love. But love marked by a different kind of reality.

There is an emotional and spiritual exhaustion caused by unending sacrifice that has nothing to do with love or commitment. This is the caregiver's affliction. The sheer routine of a life defined by the needs of the other wears one down. The support of friends and the availability of respite care—as helpful as they are—cannot remove the burden of chronic exhaustion and sadness. You learn to live with that— like a mother learns to live with a chronically sick child. But you never get used to it.

No one can live with relentless pain—be it physical, mental or spiritual. We all learn to deal with it in ways that allow us to get on with our lives. We erect barriers (Yeats' "stone"?) to protect us from being hurt more than we can bear. For me, the stone is a kind of detachment that allows me to be present to Betty, while at the same time prevents me from becoming overwhelmed by the injustice of it all. I think this is an unconscious defense mechanism I have adopted in order to keep on living. And maybe that's the point: regardless of what has happened to Betty, I must keep on living. We are born to live, and must find ways to do that. Stress, anger, rage, self-pity and impotence are destructive emotions that create havoc of their own. Because our bodies are wiser than we are, they create "escape hatches" to siphon off pent up negative energy and keep us reasonably balanced so that we can continue to live.

Stones make long sacrifices bearable. Like all defense mechanisms, from the outside they may look bad. But from the inside, it may be the only way to survive. If there is anything I have learned through this, it is that life looks completely different from the inside.

Everyone can master a grief but he that hath it.

William Shakespeare

She is permanently in the nursing facility, and I'm alone in the apartment. After fifty-two years, it has finally come to that. Living in a retirement community has reminded me that this happens to everyone sooner or later. But when it happens to you, it is different.

I don't feel sorry for me as much as I do for her. I am healthy and can get on with my life. But she is physically and mentally afflicted and has no life. All she has ever wanted was to take care of her husband, tend her garden, and have a modicum of freedom. But that was taken from her twenty years ago with the first stroke. When we came to the retirement community, loved the beauty of the surroundings and the spaciousness of our apartment. Now that, too, has been taken from her. What does she have? A semi-private room, institutional food, surrounded by infirm, demented people, and a forced dependency on nurse's aides for her bodily functions.

I visit her twice a day—a task that has become an obligation more than a desire. She is terribly lonely and wants to come home, although she knows she can't. We don't talk about it much, but I see it in her eyes. She never complains and is doing the best she can to make the best of it. But it is tough to be where you don't want to be, and know that there is no hope for parole. She does the same things in the nursing home that she did at home (watch TV and leaf through catalogues). But it's not the same. The best nursing home is not your own home. I think the difference is the sense of freedom and independence you have in your own home. You may do the

179

same things, but it's **Your** space. And that makes all the difference.

I am now a widower—not legally, but functionally. I sleep by myself, I eat breakfast by myself, I talk to myself, and I wander around the apartment by myself. For the first time in fifty-three years, I am alone. I grieve this loss. Some people are "loners." They thrive on aloneness as a way of life. I'm not that way. While I need periods of solitude, still I desire companionship. Fortunately I have my work, my music, and my friends who bring me consolation and a certain fulfillment. But none of that removes the sense of loneliness I feel when I walk into the apartment at the end of the day and nobody is there. My friends give me counsel and encouragement—all of it appreciated, and some of it helpful. But at the end of the day, I am still alone and must find my way. This is a kind of death I must face.

We now no longer attempt to change that which cannot be changed. We no longer ignore that which can be changed. And we finally have the wisdom to know the difference.

Tao Te Ching, trans. William Martin

For twenty years, I have watched my wife suffer from strokes and dementia, and have tortured myself with questions like: Why do bad things happen to good people? Why do good things happen to bad people? Why does growing old have to be so excruciating? Every day, as I walk down the corridor of the nursing facility to visit her, I am overwhelmed with sadness and dread. Sadness for what she has to live with, and dread knowing that one day I, too, will be unable to feed or toilet myself, and will have to count on the kindness of others.

But the other day, as I read William Martin's wonderful translation of the **Tao Te Ching,** I came across this verse, and suddenly realized that the questions I have been asking have no answers, and to keep on asking them is an exercise in futility and hubris.

Like Job, I have demanded answers from God. I remember the day twenty years ago when I pounded my fists so hard on the wall of the chapel at the Mayo Clinic Hospital (where she was hospitalized for her fifth brain operation) that blood dripped down the wall from my torn and bruised skin—bloody testimony of a broken and enraged man who could not fathom that God would allow a good woman to suffer that way. Over the years, I modulated my anger and learned to get on with life. But as she has become more impaired, the old questions have re-emerged—this time not with anger, but despair.

It is here that the wisdom of the Tao has helped me. The truth is that suffering is woven into the fabric of our humanity. To live is to suffer. I understand that intellectually, until the suffering touches me or mine. Then it becomes different. But the truth of the matter is, it isn't. I, too, must bow to the mysterious forces that have ordained that to know life is to know suffering. The two are inextricably linked.

Because I love her, I want to remove her suffering. But I can't. Instead, I must learn how to "no longer attempt to change that which cannot be changed." To do this requires the ancient virtues of *'docilitas'*—acquiescence to reality as it is—and humility: allowing God to have sovereignty over my life. I believe in God's love, but when the pain becomes extreme, or lasts too long, or I find the suffering utterly meaningless—then I begin to doubt. When the doubt begins, the anxiety is not far behind.

There is some suffering that is utterly meaningless. The kind for which there is neither cause nor reason, and no remedy short of death. Dementia is a good example. To try to understand why this is so, is to proceed down a dark corridor that ends in despair, for which, as Sartre wrote, there is "No Exit."

The burden has been my determination to find a meaning for her suffering, and the inability to create emotional distance from her pain so that I can continue to live. To be 'present' and 'not present' requires a balance and exercise in gentleness, patience, endurance, wisdom, docilitas, and humility. I'm a work in progress.

It is well with my soul.

Horatio Spafford

Last evening, while sitting with Betty in the Nursing Home, I asked her how she felt. To my amazement she said: "I'm happy with my life. I've made peace with who I am and where I am. And it's okay." I sat stunned, reflecting on the fact that this is a woman who over the last twenty years has suffered two strokes, a brain tumor, and five brain operations—all of which left her neurologically and cognitively handicapped. For twenty years she has required care, and is now in a nursing home because of dementia. And when asked how she is, she says: "I'm happy with my life."

Years ago I used to sing an old hymn entitled *"It Is Well With My Soul."* I haven't sung it for years. But last evening, the first stanza came back to me:

> *When sorrows like sea billows roll;*
>
> *Whatever my lot, Thou hast taught me to say*
>
> *It is well, it is well with my soul.*

The slings and arrows of outrageous fortune have wounded Betty for twenty years, and robbed her of much we take for granted. Judged from the outside, her life is barren and devoid of almost all pleasure. But alas, she has a different view of life. Though difficult, it is not devoid of pleasure and meaning. She does not understand why it all happened, but accepts it for what it is. She is convinced that there is a meaning to it all, and wants simply to do the best she can with the time and strength she has available. She refuses to analyze it. Rather, she accepts it.

Resignation is one thing; acceptance is something else. I have resigned myself to the cruelty of these last twenty years. But down deep in my heart, I have not accepted it. Betty, on the other hand, has moved beyond resignation and accepted reality as it is. In so doing, she has found a deeper meaning in her life.

In his **Testament**, St. Francis of Assisi wrote that when he kissed the leper, "What before had been nauseating to me became sweetness and life." This is what Betty has done. She has kissed the "leper" of her disability, dependence, and disfigurement, and in so doing has been freed from the suffering that comes from bitterness and anger at not living the life she thought she deserved.

It is well with her soul.

I know nothing, God, about how you think.
Your wisdom is too much for me. I cannot lift it with ideas,
thoughts to excuse you from cruelty.
I cannot flee from the challenge of it.
Dear God, do not let us suffer without explanation.
Be God so clearly, stand by us so palpably, that our
sufferings fall into perspective.

John Carmody

John Carmody was a man of God, a professor of religion at Santa Clara University, and a man dying from multiple myeloma. His book **God is No Illusion** is a wonderful collection of meditations on his journey through the valley of the shadow of death. His reflections portray a man struggling with his mortality and a desire to find meaning in his suffering. The two passages I have lifted bring his struggle into bold relief, and have come to describe where I am at this point in my journey.

After twenty-seven years of strokes, a brain tumor, multiple brain operations and dementia, Betty was struck by another stroke last month that rendered her aphasic, and last week developed a Bell's Palsy on the right side of her face. Now she not only cannot speak intelligibly, but has a paralysis of her face. It is too much for one person to bear. She no longer wants to live—and I don't blame her. This is cruelty beyond imagination.

I do not know what to do for her—or for myself. The only thing I have to offer is my presence and my prayers. Either all this is random and without meaning, or there is meaning mysteriously hidden in her pain and loss. Ten days before he died, Abraham Heschel said,

Remember that there is meaning beyond absurdity.

This sounds very much like Dietrich Bonhoeffer's prayer in prison:

I am bitter, but in thee is endurance.

I do not understand thy ways,

But thou understandeth them for me.

Both Betty and I are imprisoned. She with her overwhelming affliction, and I with the helplessness of a small child who knows not what to do or how to think about what he sees before his eyes. It is not that I don't believe. I do. Rather, it is the cruelty and (to me) the utter meaninglessness of it all. I am tempted to cry out: "Why hast thou forsaken us?" In my heart, I want to "endure." But today I am blinded by her suffering.

There are situations in which man can fulfill himself only in genuine suffering, and no other way.

Viktor Frankl

On this last day of December 2017, I look back on a year filled with suffering. Last Christmas I suffered a hypertensive cerebral hemorrhage, in May Betty died, and in November I had back surgery for a ruptured lumbar disc. Each event represented a profound loss and brought with it great physical, emotional, and spiritual suffering.

The stroke came like an earthquake: sudden, overwhelming, and terrifying. I thought I had lost everything—my mind, my speech, my ability to move, my future, my joy. Fortunately, the location of the stroke spared the motor tract and my cognitive function so that after two days I regained my speech, think properly, and move all my extremities. There has been residual brain damage (loss of taste, poor appetite, weight loss, balance disturbance, and significant short-term memory deficits) which may remain. But on balance, I am profoundly grateful for what has been spared.

I have three unforgettable memories while in the neurological ICU. The first, unspeakable spiritual pain at not feeling God's presence and comfort in my distress. I remember praying fervently for a word of comfort to sustain me in my fear and travail. But nothing came. It was all a dark void, and I felt God had abandoned me. The second, that I had been stripped of every vestige of control in my life. I had been reduced to total physical, emotional, and spiritual nakedness. Nothing I had achieved in my life—my education, my career, my academic success—mattered. At that moment, I was nothing more than a little man begging for help. That darkness and sense of abandonment persisted for months. The third, the outpouring of love and concern by so many. Through them, I saw God's love in action.

My grief at Betty's loss is only now beginning to be felt. It has been seven months since her death, and I am just now recognizing how much she had to suffer. My grief is not just at her loss; I am truly grateful that she is no longer suffering and is in God's hands. My real pain is how much and how long she had to suffer: twenty-six years of strokes and dementia, aphasia, bilateral facial nerve paralysis, vulvar sores. All the indignities and humiliation of her dependence. Throughout it all she never complained, but bore it with an acceptance born of resignation and faith. Even as I write this, I have to stop because the very thought of this fills me with tears of anger and remorse. No one should have to go through what she went through. I confess that after all this time I still have not been able to let go—standing by her bed hour after hour, week after week, month after month, year after year, watching her suffer and not being able to do anything to help. My presence was her only consolation—and my greatest pain.

You must understand that we face two types of problems in life. One kind of problem provokes the question "What are we going to do about it?" The other kind poses the subtler question "How do we behave toward it?"

T.S. Eliot

The latter type of problem resembles a mystery more than a puzzle; it demands a response that resembles a ritual repeated more than a technique.

William F. May

Most of the problems in life—moral and medical—are problems for which there are no readily available solutions. Particularly for the elderly, life is lived out "in the midst of encroaching deprivations often insoluble."

As I reflect on my own increasing disabilities (physical and mental), I am struck by T.S. Eliot's insight. He was giving a lecture to undergraduate students when a student asked him: "Mr. Eliot, what are we going to do about the problem you discussed?" Eliot replied: "You have asked the wrong question," and went on to offer the quote above.

One of the purposes of life is to find the right questions to ask. The Egyptian writer (and Nobel Laureate) Naguib Mahfouz once wrote:

You can tell whether a man is clever by his answers; you can tell whether a man is wise by his questions.

I have come to the sobering realization that each person on this earth is apportioned a mixture of joy and sorrow. The timing, mixture, and specific manifestation of this mixture remain a mystery known only to the Divine—or to chance, if one sees life as an expression of randomness. The joys of youth, physical beauty, health, striving, and accomplishment in the first half of life are undeniable. Without them, we have little to show that we made a measurable contribution to the world into which we were born.

But in the second half of life, things change. We are brought (against our will) into a stage in life in which we become aware of our mortality, our flaws, our failures, and the slow but relentless limitations of our body and mind—all of which we have no control over. These losses weigh heavy on us as we grow older. This is what Eliot was talking about. Despite the wonderful (but temporary) interventions (joint replacements, bypass surgery, dementia-slowing medication, etc.), the problem persists because the bodily parts are simply worn out. It is here that the question arises: "How do we behave toward it?"

I am taken by May's suggestion that ritual can play a vital role in responding to this question. What is ritual? It is not the same thing as "routine"—like brushing my teeth in the morning, or any other habit done on (an almost unconscious basis) as a part of daily living. By contrast, ritual is an action consciously performed for a higher (often spiritual) purpose. Every religion has its unique rituals, purposely designed to draw the communicant closer to God. Rituals may include singing, standing, bending, dancing, moving in spatial patterns, reciting sacred scripture together or alone, praying publicly or privately, remaining silent for a specific period of time, etc. Each act is performed meticulously and repetitively with a specific purpose in mind—namely, to draw closer to the Divine.

What May is suggesting is that ritual is an important tool in learning how to live with a problem that won't go away. It possesses the mysterious power to turn an enemy (our unrelenting problem) into an ally by bringing us into deeper contact with ourselves and our Creator, and thereby gaining a new and deeper perspective on the issues we are facing. On first appearance, repeating a phrase, a series of movements, or whatever makes up one's own personally developed ritual, seems irrational and even ridiculous. But thousands of years of religious practice, by millions of followers of different faith traditions, has proved its value. There is healing power in this practice.

Ritual is not a panacea. Nor is it some kind of spiritual gymnastic one can do with the hope of being freed from the problem. Rather, it is a way to live with the problem in a way which allows one to live at a deeper level of humanity. The wonderful Yiddish "benediction" **May you live till you die** is the goal of ritual.

You must give up the life you planned in order to have the life that is waiting for you. If the path before you is clear, you're probably on someone else's. The cave you fear to enter holds the treasure you seek.

Joseph Campbell

I began this book of reflections with a quote from Bernstein's "Mass" wherein the young priest, seeing the broken pane of glass, discovered that there is beauty in its brokenness. At the time I wrote that, I didn't feel like I was that broken pane of glass. Now I do. I am much older than I was then and can no longer do the things I used to. My physical strength, my memory, my ability to make rapid decisions, my mobility, my balance—all these have been taken from me and left me feeling broken and useless.

Joseph Campbell sees it differently. He is persuaded that there is another, richer dimension of life awaiting me if I can get hold of it. In other words, he calls me to change my life's paradigm.

What is my paradigm, and where did I get it? When examined closely, my self-definition comes from an educational system based on performance. I was "good" if I got A's and "not good" if I got anything less. My parents did not impose this on me. It was generated solely by an early, competitive academic environment based on "doing" rather than "being." Once that pattern was established, the path was set for replication wherever I went. I hasten to say that I am profoundly grateful for the education I received, and I honor my teachers. At the same time, there is a terrible downside to pure performance. I have since learned that any virtue overdone becomes a liability.

Over the years, that paradigm served me well. Hard work, responsibility, dedication, precision, and accomplishment are noble qualities regardless of what one does in life. I have embodied those qualities and been amply rewarded by society. But my abilities have been taken from me by age and illness and created a sense of brokenness and decrepitude. My paradigm no longer works.

Campbell offers me an antidote for two reasons:

1. He confronts me with the possibility of a meaningful life beyond my brokenness.

2. He knows I fear to enter "the cave" where I can find the treasure I seek. What is the treasure I seek? I seek meaning, beauty, and peace above all else. In order to reach that goal, I must give up my paradigm and find another more lasting and meaningful one, a paradigm appropriate for who and where I am at this time in my life.

I am beginning to see something I never saw—namely, there is beauty in brokenness. In order to experience this, I must reframe my thinking about myself: not just broken, but broken **and** beautiful. Not broken **but** beautiful. There is a world of difference. In the old paradigm, brokenness is reluctantly tolerated with beauty tacked on for compensation. Rather like dating a not-very-pretty girl and saying afterward, "But she had a nice personality." No, not like that. In the new paradigm, one recognizes that brokenness (as painful as it may be) is a necessary requirement (Campbell's "cave") for discovering a new life. And more, there is a special kind of beauty that emanates from the person who lives comfortably with his/her brokenness. Something new grows within that person and changes how they think and act. It is not a masochism that revels in the brokenness, but a gentleness that has not just accepted the inevitable, but embraced the inevitable as a preface to something mysteriously greater and more fulfilling. I fear to enter that cave. But I want to enter it. Kyrie eleison.

I shall but love thee better after death.

Elizabeth Barrett Browning, "Songs from the Portuguese"

Death is not extinguishing the light; it is putting out the lamp because the dawn has come.

Tagore

After twenty-eight years of suffering, Betty has finally been released and is at rest. It was an indescribable journey for both of us. That one person should have been burdened with a brain tumor, three strokes, five brain operations, dementia, and the final humiliation of aphasia is beyond comprehension. And what is even more incomprehensible is the grace and courage with which she bore those burdens. Never have I known anyone to suffer so much for so long.

We were married fifty-nine years, the last twenty-eight of which were consumed by her illness. She did everything they asked her to do. That was her way. Yet despite excellent medical care and her best efforts, the disease took its course until it finally claimed its victim.

As I reflect on her death, I hear the second movement of Schubert's string quartet "Death and the Maiden" in my ears. It was based on the German poet Matthias Claudius' poem of the same name: the story of a young maiden whom Death wants. She cries out that she is too young to die and begs him to leave her alone. But he refuses and finally claims her for himself. Betty was only fifty-five when she had her first stroke and a large vascular brain tumor diagnosed.

We were young, she was healthy, I was at the height of my career, we had just settled down in Hershey. And then suddenly all that changed, and I went from being a husband to being a caregiver for the next twenty-two years until she went into a nursing home and finally a dementia unit for the last four years of her life. The last year of her life was made unbearable by her aphasia. The moment she realized that she could no longer speak coherently, she died inwardly, and quickly descended into a deep dementia from which she never recovered.

Though I miss her terribly, I have accepted the biological facts of life. Neurological disease is horrible and claims its victims without remorse. Those jaws of destiny may one day claim me as it did her. The burden of pain, confusion, and anger I feel in my own heart is my own inability to accept that she had to suffer so needlessly for so many years. Few know what it is like to stand at the bedside of your beloved and see them descend into their suffering, and not be able to do anything about it. That is pure hell for the caregiver.

I have often thought about euthanasia—something I was against in my early years. But watching Betty suffer for so long without hope has changed my mind. Had it been possible, I would have made arrangements for her to be euthanized. This will shock some, I know. But they should walk in my shoes first.

I love Betty more in her death than I did before she died. Her courage, her patience, her determination to accept what is, her moral strength is beyond anything I can imagine. She never complained. What can I say? I stand in awe and reverence.

And did you get what you wanted from this life, even so?

I did.

And what did you want?

To call myself beloved, to feel myself beloved on the earth.

Raymond Carver, "Late Fragment"

I have learned to be content whatever the circumstances.

Philippians 4:11

Today I celebrated my eighty-seventh birthday. Though we take aging for granted; one hundred years ago, the average age of an adult male was forty-seven. What a difference ventilation, good nutrition, vitamins, antibiotics, and immunization make! But eighty-seven is still old. I am well into the wintertime of life and live in a retirement community where people my age die regularly.

So what do I have to say on this day? Something quite remarkable. Two years ago I wrote about contentment and said: "I have no experiential knowledge of that which all the great religions of the world are convinced is the heart of wisdom—namely to be content in the midst of decline, frailty, uncertainty, dying and death. In fact, the truly rich man is he who has come to the point of being satisfied with his lot in life, whatever it is." What was not true for me then, has become true now.

Last evening I was listening to the legendary Romanian pianist Dinu Lipatti perform a Chopin sonata, and I realized that I was in the presence of true greatness. To be in the presence of greatness is to know that you do not (nor will ever) possess such a gift, and that life is enriched by acknowledging this, and accepting the gift proffered without intimidation or competitive remorse.

After I finished listening, I had two thoughts. First, the unspeakable beauty of Chopin. And second, a surprising sense of contentment with my life. I am not Chopin, I am not Dinu Lipatti. I am me, a man of modest abilities, modest means, and modest accomplishments. So much of my life has been spent wanting to be someone I am not that I have had difficulty seeing and accepting the gifts I have been given. But somehow, listening to Chopin, I found myself thinking: "Despite my obscurity and shortcomings, I am content with who I am, where I am, and what I have been given to do." It is this realization that has made me appreciate Raymond Carver's quote—especially the two words "even so." We don't use that phrase much anymore. It means "despite everything" or "nevertheless." In today's jargon, it would read: "Despite everything, did you get what you wanted?"

What struck me was his answer: "I did." That is, despite all the falls, frustrations, failures, disappointments, and heartbreaks: "I did." And more, when asked what it was he really wanted, he said "I really wanted to be loved." How profound is that! If you know you are loved you can survive the falls, failures, disappointments and heartbreaks. I'm reminded of Aristotle's comment: "He who is not loved seeks to be admired."

Carver's experience has been my experience also. The painful "even so's" of my own journey have slowly found an acceptance (even though not always a meaning) because I know that I am loved. And so, at this late date in my life, despite all the unfulfilled dreams and fantasies, I can say that I got what I really wanted. And what did I want? To be fully loved for who I am in the fullness of my humanity.

Contentment, as simple as it sounds, is a complex idea. Does it come with age? Not necessarily. Is it a steady state in the sense of once you "have it" your problems will go away? No. Is it something you can create by sheer effort? No. As a matter of fact, the harder you try to get it, the more elusive it becomes.

Contentment, as I know it to be, is not so much a "fixed-point" which one arrives at—like mastering a skill after years of effort. Rather, it is a grace given at moments when one least expects it. A quiet, almost inaudible voice that places life in a different perspective—a kind of existential reframing that allows us to see our journey in a different light. The hallmark is its unexpectedness. It is "given" to us and not something we can produce or work our way into.

I know that my "Chopin moment" will not immunize me from the "slings and arrows of outrageous fortune." Such are the "givens" of life, part of our humanity, and cannot be side-stepped. But I also know that I have been granted a perspective that can serve as a counterbalance in the midst of the storms of life. I do believe that the Apostle Paul discovered a secret that held his chaotic life together when he declared that he had learned how to be content regardless of where he was and under whatever circumstances he found himself. That lesson had to be learned and practiced in order to make it a part of his psychic and spiritual reality. So when my storms burst in upon me, I must remember my moment of centeredness so that I don't get carried with fear, doubt, and anger—which are sadly my default reactions when things don't go well.

I also suspect that contentment is the fruit of the second half of life and is not achievable in the first half of life. This is a mystery only because one might well argue that something as important as contentment should be available in the first half of life also. But I don't think this is possible or even desirable. The first half of life is given over to learning, skill training, stretching and being stretched, striving and achieving, learning how to negotiate the uncertainties of life, and earning the scars of a warrior. Only much later can one look back, search for the threads of meaning, and open oneself to a deeper perspective of what life is all about. Success comes quickly; wisdom takes a lifetime.

I am grateful for the gift of contentment. It has allowed me to say "yes" to myself and to my tiny place in the universe. It has not answered any of the burning questions of the world in which I live. I know that. But that's okay. In some way I have found a pearl of great price which has given me hope and peace. I dare not ask for more.

Epilogue

What our life amounts to,
at least for those who reach full age,
is largely, if not entirely,
a matter of what we become within.

Dallas Willard

I have come to the end of my reflections and wonder if I reached my goal. What was my goal? It was not to tell a story, but rather to explore, in as open and honest a way as possible, one man's journey into a hitherto unknown realm—the world of aging. Looking back on my choice of aphorisms, I am struck by the recurrence of certain themes: the complexity and fear of aging, the loss of a life partner, the consequences of physical disability, coming to grips with death and dying, learning how to grow old gracefully, and finally, the struggle to find meaning in physical and mental decline.

I have borrowed a profound quote from Dallas Willard, late Professor of Philosophy at my alma mater, the University of Southern California, because it summarizes, in a beautiful way, what I believe is the purpose of old age—and hence the purpose of this little book. At the end of our lives, we are more than the things we did, the places we lived, and the events that came upon us. The ancient saying, "The whole is greater than the sum of the parts," is apt and true. We are more than our gains and losses. We are who and what we have become in our hearts. The hallmark of a life well lived is the ability to transcend our losses, our heartbreaks, and our pain, and find meaning and beauty in our lives as we are in the here and now.

To do this requires great courage, patience, a determination not to give up when we find ourselves oppressed by the dark night of the soul, and an abiding faith that we can continue to grow and find joy and meaning in our journey.

Maybe Maya Angelou was right when she said that most people don't grow up, they just grow old. I don't know. I know only three things: 1) growing old is difficult 2) it is possible to find meaning in the aging process and 3) getting there is the hard part.

My journey may not be yours. Even so, I hope these thoughts and insights will be of some help along the way.

About the Author

George Simms is a retired physician and former Chairperson of the Department of Family and Community Medicine in the Penn State University College of Medicine. He received his M.D. from the University of Zurich, Switzerland Faculty of Medicine, a Ph.D. in Human Behavior from the United States International University, and a Master in Theological Studies from Harvard Divinity School. He is the founding Hospice Medical Director at the Masonic Village Elizabethtown, Pennsylvania. He currently resides at the Masonic Village.

Made in the USA
Monee, IL
30 November 2024

aaaca760-2ca2-4973-91da-1e9d7b8cfd7eR01